The LINGUIST and
the EMPEROR

The LINGUIST and the EMPEROR

NAPOLEON and CHAMPOLLION'S QUEST to DECIPHER the ROSETTA STONE

Daniel Meyerson

BALLANTINE BOOKS　NEW YORK

A Ballantine Book
Published by The Random House Publishing Group
Copyright © 2004 by Daniel Meyerson

Ballantine and colophon are registered trademarks of Random House, Inc.

www.ballantinebooks.com

LIBRARY OF CONGRESS CATALOGING-IN-PUBLICATION DATA

Meyerson, Daniel.
The linguist & the emperor : Napoleon and Champollion's quest to decipher the
Rosetta stone / by Daniel Meyerson.
p. cm.
ISBN 0-345-45067-1
1. Rosetta stone. 2. Egyptian language—Writing, Hieroglyphic. 3. Champollion,
Jean-François, 1790–1832. 4. Napoleon I, Emperor of the French, 1769–1821.
I. Title: Linguist and the emperor. II. Title.

PJ1531.R5M49 2004
493'.1'092—dc22   2003065515

Manufactured in the United States of America

First Edition: March 2004

1 3 5 7 9 10 8 6 4 2

Book design by Jo Anne Metsch

Dedicated to:

Mollie Snitovsky, fantast, painter, and poet,
who taught me that it is part of the
probable that the improbable will occur.

And

Nancy Miller, Wilde's *Critic as Artist*—
de vrai touche. For entering so completely
(and brilliantly) into the world of this book.

And

the forty-two Egyptian gods of the dead
(among whom rages my agent, Noah Lukeman).

Acknowledgments

Heartfelt thanks to:

Rosalie Kaufman, whose friendship I value and without whose New York hospitality this book would not have been written.

Mosin Rashidi, connoisseur, for his extraordinary Egyptian hospitality and for patiently answering endless questions.

Dan Smetanka, who looked at those first sketchy pages and believed. For his encouragement and enthusiasm over months which stretched into years.

Mary Gow of Brooklyn Museum's Wilburforce Egyptian Library: the woman who knows too much.

Sylvia Levy of Here's a Book Store! for credit, encouragement, and much kindness.

Acknowledgments

Leah: *Maa'-hru,* "true of voice."

Dr. Shoshannah—for friendship.

Ahnkeroot, Connie Skedgell, and Prof. Maura Spiegal—
for careful reads and strong responses.

Bubi Scholz, European Master, Middle Weight, 1964, for
inspiration.

Gene Mydlowski and Beck Stvan of Ballantine Books for
the knockout cover!

Vivian Heller, marvelous fellow writer.

Deirdre Lanning for her endless patience and help.

Contents

Contents

The LINGUIST and the EMPEROR

Prelude

IN HIS HOVEL, the linguist dreams of the emperor, of the one who commands with a wave of his hand. He dreams of power and the freedom it confers.

On his throne, the emperor dreams of the linguist, of the one who understands. He dreams of knowledge and the meaning it confers.

And who are they, this improbable pair?

Does it matter? They are eternal types who have always existed and who always will.

Call the emperor "Alexander the Great" if you like. Young, handsome, in the first flush of power, he is just grown out of boyhood and already master of Greece. Surrounded by his followers, he seeks out Diogenes. He rides to the hills above Athens, sees the bald old philosopher lying naked on the ground and greets him:

"I am Alexander."

"I am Diogenes, the dog."

"The dog?"

"I bark at the greedy and bite stupid louts."

A murmur goes through the crowd of soldiers and hangers-on, but Alexander continues, unfazed: "Ask what you will of me! Whatever you request is yours."

"This is what you can do for me," the old man shouts: "Get out of my light!"

And Alexander, thus rebuked, turns away and says with awe: "If I were not Alexander, I would be Diogenes!"

His soldiers are scandalized. His admiration for such figures is something they will never understand. Rough, brave men, they deride the scholars Alexander takes with him everywhere. What great deeds have these parasites performed, what battles have they fought to be so honored? When Alexander conquers Egypt, he sets them the futile task of unraveling its mysteries, inscriptions written in signs half-forgotten even then. And they are with him again in Babylon, these puny-armed men with their bald pates, and in the east when the young hero weeps because there are no more worlds to conquer. It is a grief his scholars will never know, for their realm is limitless, as infinite as thought.

Grudgingly, the warriors protect these "camp followers," these hangers-on who serve no discernible purpose. But the emperor commands it and it is not for them to complain.

Not then, and not some two thousand years later when another emperor called Napoleon sets out for Egypt with 167 scholars, the finest minds of France, stowed away on his warships. Poets, mathematicians, and architects, they sling their hammocks among crates of dry biscuit and rows of mounted guns.

Though they will accomplish much in Egypt, meticulously sketching and measuring and recording, the scholar who will make the greatest use of all this knowledge is not among them.

He is still a child.

It is early in the story—Year VII by the calendar of the revolutionaries which dates not from the birth of a Savior but from the triumph of freedom and the guillotine. It is the month of "Floreal," Flowers, the name these stern men have given to May not for sentimental reasons—what are spring and love to them?—but rather to invoke Nature, the goddess of their pitiless cause.

Floreal Year 7: May 1798. Not yet a linguist, Champollion is only a boy who is punished for being moody and disobedient. And the emperor is not yet emperor, but only a certain General Bonaparte on his way to conquer Egypt for the glory of France.

They are both still young but what they will achieve is as palpable to them as a chill running down their spines or the scent of the flowers of that revolutionary spring.

"I felt the earth spin away from me as if I were flying in the sky!" Bonaparte declares at his first taste of battle. In ecstasy, he stands amid the dying and the dead, transfixed by a premonition of what the future holds.

And like Napoleon, Champollion anticipates, intuits his fate. "I will decipher the hieroglyphs!" the eleven-year-old cries at his first sight of the mysterious writing, running his hand over the coffin of a young girl who had died thousands of years before.

For both linguist and emperor, it is the beginning. They can feel the future rushing to them; the glory that will be theirs. But with this glory will be great suffering, great disillusion, and great despair. It is early but they will never again be as happy as they are now, standing at the threshold of the future and peering through the mysterious door.

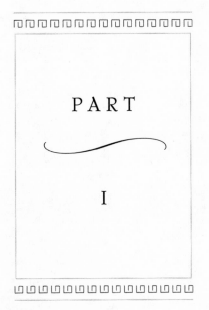

PART

I

Chapter One

Ab Ovo—
From the Egg

abcdΦΧΨΩυˀ כ٦לٸ Ι Ƴㅜㅠㅁㄴㅣ ﾌ ρή έ ῦβdefghoטգ ʂγ ɯ ग्गa б μ λ ξ θ η δ β ʃ {ʊ ĩ ι stuv ɟ ¡
ﻭ ٻﺀ ﺓ ﺕ ﺙ ﺝ ﺡ ﺥ ﺩ ﺫ ﺭ ﺯ ﺱ ﺵ ﺹ ﺽ ﻁ ﻅ ﻉ ﻍ ﻑ ﻕ ﻙwxyz ل ﻡ ﻥ ﻩ hijklmn ﻭ ﻯ ﺍ ﺏ ﺝ ﺩ ﻩ ﻭ ﺍ ﺭ ﻕ ﺭ ﻱ ﻱ ˮ opqr

FIGEAC. 1792. At the height of that violent phe-
nomenon known as the Great Fear, violent bands roam the
French countryside. Taking advantage of the disorder, they
steal what they can, destroying whatever comes in their
path like a force of nature. They set fire to humble farms as
well as to great Chateaux, murdering, raping, choosing
their victims from poor and rich alike. In a once-idyllic
town in the south of France, the vineyards and fields are set
ablaze and its Benedictine monastery is ransacked by a mob
that has battered down its great bronze doors. Monks are
tortured to make them reveal the hiding place of rumored

9

treasure—while the pillagers ignore the finest prize: the books of the monastery's great library.

The Abbé, a renowned scholar, has thrown some of the rarest volumes into a sack. One of them is a huge gilded work published during the Renaissance but written much earlier, in the fourth century AD: Horapollo's *Hieroglyphs,* the only ancient work devoted to the mystery of Egyptian writing. The Abbé, a vigorous monk in his sixties, is determined to escape not only with his life, but with some of the treasures from this silent place of study. As the mob breaks into the fortresslike building, the holy man, together with a novice, makes his way through secret tunnels beneath the monastery. He emerges into the night with a plan. It is to the house of Champollion, the bookseller, that the monk flees. Champollion will prize his learning, the Abbé fervently hopes. And yes, Champollion takes the refugee in at the risk of his life and so acquires a tutor for his older son.

There are two boys, twelve years apart. The monk will teach the older son. The other, Jean François, is too young for lessons. But despite this fact—perhaps because of the fact that he is a child—he will be the one most affected by the Abbé. For during the years Jean François grows up, the monk is a powerful presence in the household. Every day, the boy listens to him secretly celebrating mass in a low voice. The shutters are closed and the servants are sent away on a pretext. It is a time when everything associated with the old regime, including its religion, is risky. The mystery of the Catholic ritual, intensified by danger, greatly moves the sensitive boy. These secret masses are some of his most profound memories.

It is from the Abbé that Jean François hears the story that will obsess him, something the old man tells him by chance one day. The two are walking through the damp stone corridors of the house, which are lined with piles and piles of books. The boy, who is five, notices one of the books opened to an engraving. He questions the old man about it.

The Abbé explains that the bearded man with his arms flung out is the king Belshazzar, a wicked ruler whose father had destroyed the Temple in Jerusalem. The picture portrays Belshazzar in the middle of a great feast. Blaspheming the God of Israel, he is eating and drinking from the sacred Temple vessels when suddenly a disembodied hand writes mysterious words on the wall. These words fill the king with fear: *Mene, mene, tekel, upharsin.* No one among the king's sages can decipher the words, the Abbé continues, until finally Daniel, a Hebrew youth carried into exile, is brought before the assembly. With a glance Daniel succeeds in interpreting the words.

" '*Mene, mene, tekel, upharsin*—You have been weighed in the balance and found wanting,' " the Abbé repeats Daniel's explanation. But in the nightmares that plague the boy for years afterward, it is not Daniel but he, Jean François, who is called upon to interpret the strange words. He is threatened by the king's soldiers with suffering and death, but the writing remains a mystery and the boy awakens in a sweat.

This is the striking picture of Jean François which the Abbé records: a child crying out in the dark, jumping from bed and running through the book-crammed corridors of a gloomy house looking for someone, anyone, to console him because he cannot decipher inscrutable words.

⊓ ⊓ ⊓

AS A CHILD, he does not play.

In the center of the square in Figeac there is a guillotine. And on the roof of a house near Champollion's—high up, amid the drying clothes and stacks of firewood—there is another fashioned from planks of wood and a chair: "Vile aristocrats!" the children shout as they push their "victims" forward. "Damned and guilty race! In the name of liberty, die!"

"One more moment, Monsieur the Executioner!" a young girl cries as she struggles to break free, crossing herself and falling to her knees. "*Encore un moment!*" she pleads, pretending to be Madame Du Barry on the scaffold. For the mistress of Louis XV has just been executed and her last words have become a cruel joke in a death-obsessed land.

Young Champollion is not recruited for such games. He is too dreamy or else—his other side—he is too wild and hot-tempered to go along with any game made up by others. The children reject the swarthy boy with his large dark eyes and shock of black hair and intense expression. And he turns from them as well, going his own way.

His father is never home. In times such as these, it is not easy for a bookseller to thrive. People prefer a pair of shoes or a scrawny chicken to books. A side of meat is more to the point than the wisdom of the Greeks or heavy volumes from the church fathers.

Learning is suspect. The great chemist Lavoisier is sent to death with the jeer, *The Revolution has no need of you!* Naturalist, historian, philosopher—all die to the same refrain. The mathematician Condorcet, despite his revolutionary fervor, is hunted like a wild animal. Found hiding in the countryside, shunned by his friends, bearded and in rags, he still pathetically clutches his manuscript, *Sketch of a Historic Table of the Progress of the Human Spirit,* a work he will take with him to the scaffold. It is a time not for philosophy, but for action. And so, Champollion père, impoverished bookseller, takes to the roads.

Jean François' mother, crippled by rheumatism, spends her days at a window overlooking the narrow stone courtyard. Even before the revolution, she had withdrawn from the world. Unable to read or write, as superstitious as a witch, she puts her faith in the Gypsies and wandering sorcerers who have brought about the miracle. For how else but with their help could it have come to pass that she—a sickly, enervated woman of forty-six, she, who had spent her days preparing for death—had given birth to a strapping, healthy son? And it is because of this mystery that, to her, the life of Jean François seems precarious. It hangs by the thread of her amulets and charms. Fearfully, she watches her son grow. When he visits her sickroom, she clutches Jean François to her, weeping and praying over him with an anguish which oppresses the boy.

Set against his mother's dark fears and passions, his father's books seem to offer light. But it is a light denied Jean François—for though he is now eight years old, he still cannot read. His education has been completely neglected. The Abbé who had taught his brother has long since fled the country. His brother Jacques, the only one to whom Jean François can turn during this torturous time, has been sent away to help support the family. He has left Figeac for Grenoble, a city five hours distant, to work there as a clerk, sending his meager earnings home.

Jean François is on his own with two examples always before him. To be a man is to read, to live by reason, by the books which fill every corner and passageway. Not to read is to be a woman, to dwell in a feverish world of fears and dreams. His mother, shut in by the four walls of her sickroom, lives a life that is not fully human.

Still, she is not a figure who can be simply dismissed. If she were, there would be no *danger,* Jean François would not have to flee so frantically from her example.

This becomes the riddle of his youth: His mother's illiteracy is both the source of her degradation and the source of her power. With her spells and her prayers, she is in touch with the mysteries of the universe, or so it seems to the boy. The forces of life and death join in mumbled incantations.

It is as if fate thrusts Jean François toward his mother's illiteracy, tormenting him and goading him to fight back. And he does fight back: fiercely. He struggles to teach himself to read. He draws the letters of the alphabet as if he were sketching pictures, covering page after page with words which have no meaning for him. And then one day, frustrated by the impenetrability of the writing, he shatters the glass cover of one of his father's bookcases. And then he shatters another, wreaking destruction until a horrified servant comes running and beats him into stopping.

⊓ ⊓ ⊓

SOON AFTER THIS, he catches his first glimpse of Egypt.

A wandering troupe of Cathedral mimes and puppeteers visits Figeac. A tent is pitched at the edge of town and a crier announces in the square: *"The story of Thaïs of Egypt! And of the blessed St. Mark! And of Flowers of the desert! St. Moses the Black! St. Anthony! Children of the wilderness! Martyrs of Egypt! Stories of the Thebaid where our first monks sought God!"*

From time immemorial, such troupes have performed in the great cathedrals of France: passion plays, sacred dramas, scenes from the lives of the saints. But since the revolution, Christianity is out of fashion. There is a Festival of the Supreme Being and pageants honoring the Goddess of Reason, but these medieval legends are politically dangerous. And so the troupe is reduced to traveling about the countryside, finally arriving in the small provincial city of Figeac where the crier fills the air with the names of Egyptian saints and monks long dead and miracle-working hermits; a long list to which the manager makes sure the crier adds, as a "draw":

And the holy martyr Napoleon!

It is a clever ploy since General Napoleon's name is on everyone's lips just now. He has just become the "Savior of Revolution." Against all odds, he has defeated the armies of the pro-monarchist Austrians in Italy before they had a chance to attack the new republic on French soil. What does it matter that the Napoleon of the play is not a general but a martyr who died in Egypt fifteen hundred years before? It is impossible to mistake the contemporary allusion and there actually is a connection between the two Napoleons: The young Corsican general was named after the saint (or after an uncle who was named after him which the clever manager of the troupe decides is the same thing).

The manager's instincts are good: The tent is quickly packed with a crowd of the curious, among them Jean François and his brother Jacques, who has returned home for a visit. Garishly painted backdrops are arranged on the torch-lit stage and, with a clash of cymbals, Jean François is transported to a desert valley, all sand and sky.

A voice from behind the flimsy scenery calls out: "Behold Paphnutius, a monk famed for his holy life! Behold an angel who dwells on earth . . ."

There is a rustling of chains as a tall, gaunt figure—naked but for hair shirt and irons—crawls onto the stage. In the shadows thrown by the torches, his every gesture is magnified tenfold.

"Behold how he subdues his flesh!"

People cry out as he whips himself in a frenzy. He is soon covered with blood (whether his own or that of a slaughtered animal is a professional secret). Finally he throws himself on the ground to sleep.

A screen descends on which a beautiful woman is painted, her face hidden in her hands, her half-naked body turned toward the dreaming monk.

"It is the unhappy courtesan Thaïs! Save her! Oh, save her, Paphnutius!"

Getting to his feet, Paphnutius marches across the stage as the backdrops are changed for Alexandria, a worldly city famed for its philosophers and poets and whores.

But Jean François does not see the rest of the play: how Paphnutius converts Thaïs; how he brings her to the desert where the harsh life of penance kills her; and how the monk loses his faith afterward, tormented by his lust for the beautiful saint he has created . . .

The boy is in another world: He has fainted dead away from excitement. Slung like a sack of potatoes over his brother's shoulder, he is carried out into the cold night air.

And this is symbolic of what their relationship will be throughout their lives. Jean François, volatile and passionate with the excitability of a visionary, will have much trouble making his way in the world. Jacques, less inspired, will be his brother's mainstay and support, always believing in him and overlooking his moodiness and fits of temper.

Even physically the two present a contrast, Jacques having none of his brother's exotic looks. He is a large, thickset young man, with regular features and eyes heavy with learning; having been forced to give up his formal studies, he pursues them on his own late into the night, immersing himself in Greek and Latin and Hebrew. What he lacks in brilliance, he makes up in devotion. His head filled with Plato and Homer and Virgil and the Bible, Jacques staggers to work in the morning, sitting all day recording how many bolts of cloth have been sold and how much money has been collected and how much is owed. He dreams of escape.

But escape is impossible during the Terror. During the Terror, *nothing* is possible—except for violence.

The Champollions: would-be scholar Jacques, sitting on his clerk's stool in Grenoble; undisciplined, unschooled Jean François going his dreamy, solitary way; bankrupt bookseller Champollion *père;* and invalid Champollion *mère.* They are all lucky simply to be alive.

⌐⌐ ⌐⌐ ⌐⌐

A NEW WORLD is being born. If its birth pangs are inseparable from the death agonies of its enemies, so much the
worse for them! Thus proclaims the "midwife"—Robespierre the "Incorruptible"—a skillful orator whose stirring
speeches have helped him seize power (a power maintained
with denunciations and spies and fanatic scoundrels). The
flesh holds no interest for Robespierre. He is a celibate, tortured torturer, a compiler of execution lists, and, when the
mood is upon him, a maker of exquisite lace.

Day by day, citizens are arrested to satisfy the bloodlust
and morbid suspicions of the Incorruptible. Among them is
a sensual Creole named Rose who will play a large role in
the events that follow. Daily, Rose expects arrest, so when
it finally comes, she cries out with anguish, "I have done
nothing! Nothing! I am from the Americas—an innocent
woman!" She clutches her two children, a girl of ten and a
boy of twelve, as she is dragged from a small house just outside Paris.

What she says is true: She was raised on the island of
Martinique and in poverty, too, on a half-abandoned sugar
plantation ruined by hurricanes. Yet these circumstances do
not save her. She is thrown into a Paris prison with her husband, a rich aristocrat she married when she was fifteen.

Then Rose had been a girl filled with romantic dreams, sent to Paris to repair the family's fortunes. But her new husband quickly disillusioned her, despising her provincial manners and her innocence. Debauched and sated with all manner of pleasures, he has only a technical, legal interest in the young Creole brought from the islands: Without a wife he cannot inherit the family estate.

By the time of the Terror, Rose has had two children with him. She is in her early thirties. Since her arrest, her teeth have become bad, her complexion has begun to coarsen, and her clothes have gotten ragged. After her husband is guillotined, she takes what she thinks will be a last lover in prison. Something about her fascinates men; her beauty is a sum greater than its parts. And when this lover is guillotined as well, she takes *another* last lover. What sense is there in waiting for death alone? Besides which, a pregnancy would mean a nine-month reprieve. A lie will win her four at the least. Such is her reasoning as she desperately seeks niches and corners where she and her friend can steal a moment alone: in the chapel of the convent turned prison, beneath a winding staircase, even the women's privy provides a brief chance. A guard finally discovers Rose and her would-be savior in flagrante delicto, and drags them off to different cells.

Though she will not become pregnant, Rose will end up cheating the executioner. She will live to fascinate many other "last lovers," including a younger man. The most ardent of her lovers, he and his passion will both frighten and amuse her. This serious and brooding soldier will one day rename her "Josephine" and make her empress of France.

For the time being, though, Napoleon is unaware of Rose's existence. "I have only one passion, only one mistress and that is France. I sleep with her," he says grandly, taking up his first military command with a good conscience. What is the Terror to him? "The revolution?" He shrugs with a soldier's realism. "It is an opinion with bayonets." If he is a member of Robespierre's party, it is only because it is useful for him.

But even the Terror must finally come to an end. It is in the nature of things: Sooner or later, violence turns in upon itself. On the very day that Josephine is supposed to die, Robespierre, who has grown increasingly out of touch with reality, makes a fatal speech. "I fear impure influences . . . from impure men," he tells the National Assembly, staring at face after face with an intense gaze whose significance is quickly understood. "My nearest colleagues, the Committee for Public Safety itself must be purified." At first there is silence, but suddenly there are cries of "Murderer!" "Criminal!" "Tyrant!" A flood of rage is released.

The next day, Robespierre himself is dragged to the guillotine. His jaw has been broken during his attempt to escape. As he is forced onto the scaffold, he snarls and strikes out. The blade descends and his severed head is held up to the crowd. A deafening shout echoes in the Place de la Revolution. The great orator has fallen silent forever.

A time of abandoned celebration follows, a time when everything is possible. Society women walk bare-breasted across Paris on a bet. Young men, *les incroyables,* strut about in fantastic get-ups while young women take to wearing gauzy, transparent dresses that would have outraged Republican virtue just a year before. And macabre *bals du guillotine* are given, in which the revelers dance wildly, making the jerky motions of a decapitated body as the horrors of the Terror are forgotten in fountains of wine.

In the midst of the frantic merrymaking, an awkward young man in a field uniform stands silently.

"His face is thin and pale. He is contemptuous in his bearing. He has none of the qualities of the men of the study or of society," a shrewd observer (Mme. de Staël) remembers him. "If he recounts his personal experiences, he discloses the lively imagination of an Italian. Character, mind, speech—all have a strange stamp. This very strangeness helps him to win over the French . . ."

Though he has been fighting for France, Napoleon is not a Frenchman. He is from Corsica, a rugged island off the coast of Italy where blood feuds and an exaggerated code of honor formed him—and where gentry such as the Bonapartes are almost as poor as the peasants.

Sent on a scholarship to France, to the royal military academy at Brienne, young Napoleon is taunted by his aristocratic classmates for his Italian accent and his poverty. But he is a scrapper, willful and stubborn. His sense of himself only becomes stronger during his years at the academy, first at Brienne and then in the *École Militaire* in Paris where he concentrates on mathematics and artillery.

If he is an outsider, though, what sets him apart is not so much his background, his foreign birth, and poverty: it is his *consciousness.* A fellow Corsican, Paoli, sums him up, "There is nothing modern about you, Napoleon. You are straight out of Plutarch." True: It is from classical readings that Napoleon derives inspiration. Such figures as Julius Caesar and Alexander the Great stir his imagination with visions of a godlike glory and make him dissatisfied with anything less.

Which is why he stands silent and brooding at the *bal du guillotine.* Ambition gnaws at him, only made sharper by his first taste of victory. For though he has shown himself brave and a bold strategist during the early days of the revolution, what has he done, after all? Relieved a French port, Toulon, from foreign occupation. On the world-historical scale of his vast imagination, it is barely worth noticing.

What would Caesar or Alexander or . . . ? A wine glass is placed in his hand and a friend taps him on the arm. The preoccupied and abstracted soldier finds himself face-to-face with the Creole woman Rose, rescued from prison and on the arm of the Director Barras, one of the five men who now rule France.

"You should know each other: You are both from islands," the director laughs, "and you both know how to fight . . ."

Rose is about to say something pleasant and move on, but something silences her in the look Napoleon gives her: a serious and imploring and strange look very out of place in that setting.

From the beginning, everything about Rose touches him to the quick. Napoleon will remember his first impression of her with pain even after it is all over, after they have both betrayed each other and he is a defeated and exiled emperor on his prison island writing his memoirs. At this momentous meeting, her laughter is shot through with melancholy. Her abandon—her dress is very revealing—somehow has an innocence about it. Not a girlish innocence. At the time she is womanly and is more experienced, more so than he, with his one or two abrupt experiments in the physical act of love and his romantic sighing over interchangeable women. Her innocence, he decides, doesn't depend on her experience or lack thereof, but on a kind of radical purity of soul.

Though Rose is Barras' mistress, the director has already begun to tire of her. She is willing to receive Napoleon's attentions. Soon he calls on her and she quickly becomes everything to him. She finds him strange, a diversion, though somewhat oppressive—abrupt, serious, romantic, often silent, unsmiling. He is the opposite of the pleasure-loving, worldly Barras, and the opposite of herself. Rose—soon to be transformed into Josephine by the importunate soldier—thinks no more of changing her lovers than of changing her shoes.

After their first night together, Napoleon writes to her, "I have awakened full of you. The memory of last night has given my senses no rest . . . Sweet and incomparable Josephine, what an effect you have on my heart! I send you thousands of kisses—but don't kiss me. Your kisses sear my blood."

And Josephine profitably sells Napoleon's letters to the chief of police Fouché, who spies on all figures of any political importance, among whom he counts the "hero of Toulon," a man whose victory has already earned him a measure of fame.

Napoleon wants to marry Rose quickly, before he goes off to battle. She agrees, after consulting with Barras. He feels Napoleon shows promise. Moreover, Barras tells her that he intends to put Napoleon in charge of the revolutionary army languishing in the Alps.

But just who it is she is marrying, she has no more idea

of now than when she saw him silent and brooding at the Directory ball.

His Italian campaigns will do more than make him a hero and a demigod in France. They will astonish the world. Given command of a ragged army that has been languishing for months in the Italian Alps, Napoleon inspires them with his own strength of will: "Soldiers, you are hungry and almost naked," he tells the cold, half-starved men, immediately forging a mystic bond with them. "I will lead you into the most fertile plains on earth . . . There you shall find honor, glory, riches. Soldiers of Italy, can resolution fail you now?"

And he makes good on his promises. Combining brilliant tactics with desperate courage, Napoleon turns this side-theater of the war into the main one. One after the other, he defeats the superior Austrian armies sent against him. He forces the Austrians to sue for peace. He fills the empty coffers of the Directory with tribute and he searches through the churches and palaces of Italy to send the finest works of art back to France.

This means nothing to him. "What I have accomplished so far will earn me a footnote in history," he tells his adjutant. He craves much more. Like Caesar, like Alexander, he wants immortality. He decides, after much agonizing, that he will look for it in the sands of Egypt.

□ □ □

IT IS THE place their paths will cross imaginatively, Napoleon's and that of Jean François. They will sit and talk about Egypt the way two men talk who have loved the same woman. But not yet. For first Napoleon must conquer it. And Jean François must learn how to read.

Napoleon steps onto the world stage from nowhere. He appears suddenly: a gaunt, passionate young man filled with nervous energy and in love with glory. "What is happiness?" he asks in his diary during his student days. "It is the possibility of making full use of one's powers."

During the monarchy, such happiness is beyond his reach. Under Louis XVI, aristocratic birth is everything, merit nothing. Because he is a commoner, Napoleon was given an insignificant command when he completed his studies, and that is all he could expect in the future as well. And so he suffered. His genius stifled, his aggression turned inward and he wanted to die: "I see no place for myself in this world," the young officer writes to his brother. "If this continues, I shall end by not stepping aside when a carriage rushes past."

The revolution changes everything. France is attacked on all sides by monarchs fearful of her radical example. For their part, the leaders of the revolution welcome war. They understand that if their revolution does not spread to other countries, it will die. War is a necessity.

But the French army is in disarray. Its aristocratic officers have fled for their lives, leaving the rabble without a leader. Thus Destiny, in which Napoleon believes with a perfect and pagan faith, has opened the way for him.

Destiny, glory, immortality—Napoleon conceives of war in grand, heroic terms, as if he were an ancient warrior and not an artillery officer in the nineteenth century, trained in the latest, most scientific methods. This is a paradox at the heart of his character: This most realistic of realists is never disillusioned by the horrors of war. For him, it will always be what the Greek philosopher Heraclitus calls it—a saying Napoleon scribbles in the margins of an order for the day, on the back of a letter from his mother, across a bill from Josephine's dressmaker—"War, the father of all good things."

From his first campaign to his last, all he sees is glory: in Italy, where he orders that all the boys and men in a village be shot to discourage guerrilla fighting; in Egypt, where his soldiers go mad from thirst, chasing after mirages in the desert and killing themselves; in the Holy Land, where the ravages of the plague force him, out of mercy, to poison his own men; during the long Russian retreat where it is common to see starving men throw themselves on a fallen horse and devour its flank and liver while the animal is still alive.

And even when he *is* shaken, he forces himself to overcome his weakness. Looking over a battlefield where thousands lie dying and dead, he turns away and murmurs, "The corpse of an enemy always smells sweet,"—the words of a Roman emperor he is pretending to be. The next moment he will be some other Roman or Greek, another figure whose words, whose stance, he has made his own. When he becomes emperor, he will stride through the palace with a swaying gait after hearing that Louis XVI walked in this manner. Even his physical maladies are viewed by him as "world-historical": Is it Nature that has afflicted him with epilepsy or is he unconsciously mimicking that other great epileptic, Julius Caesar?

Is Napoleon a man afflicted with disease or one suffering from a superabundance of life and imagination and nervous energy? A revolutionary or an autocrat? Is he a Frenchman—when his troops grumble at the hardships in Egypt, he curses the French, *a nation that makes love with its mouth and fights with its feet*—or an Italian?

When alone, this revolutionary emperor, this Italian creator of French glory, does he himself know who he is?

Chapter Two

The Awakening

JEAN FRANÇOIS DISCOVERS who he is by reading.

His brother Jacques begins to teach him on visits home: first the alphabet, then everything. To begin with, he reads stories of the games on Olympus, of wrestling and discus throwing and racing. Some passages Jacques reads to the unathletic and uncoordinated boy include tales of incredible strength:

> Polydamas strangled a lion with his bare hands, a feat depicted on his statue at Olympia. He also stopped a chariot dead in its tracks, seizing hold of it as it sped past him.

First he recites in Greek, letting Jean François hear the music of the language before Jacques translates. He trans-

THE LINGUIST AND THE EMPEROR

lates not only their language, but the stories' spirit—not a physical, but a metaphysical spirit.

What are they striving for, these poised and beautiful athletes?

Victory!

But what is Victory?

It is the holy mingling of god and man.

Jacques teaches Jean François to hear the echoes of an ancient world, showing him what, at Olympus, is at stake.

Glaukos was a farmer. One day the ploughshare came away from the plough and his father saw him hammering it back with his bare fist. Impressed, the old man decided to take him to the next Olympic games. This he did but Glaukos was inexperienced and took many blows in the early bouts. When he came to his last opponent, he was so badly wounded that everybody thought he would have to give up. But his father called: "My son! Remember the ploughshare!" Whereupon Glaukos hit his opponent so hard that the contest was ended there and then.

The two brothers make a strange picture: sitting on the banks of the fetid canal that runs by the local tannery, walking through the winding streets of Figeac or in the meadows beyond the town, both lost in a dream.

On the road to sacred Olympia, there is a rocky mountain with high cliffs. It is a law that any woman discovered at the Olympic games will be thrown from this mountain. Kallipateira, though, the daughter of a famous boxer whose father and husband were both dead, disguised herself as a trainer and brought her son Pisirodos to Olympia to compete in the games. He won, and forgetting herself, his mother joyously leapt over the barrier, revealing herself to be a woman. But the authorities forgave her, passing a law that trainers, like athletes, must be naked.

Jean François becomes alive to language, discovering how a single word can throw a veil over reality—

Alcibiades, as a desperate measure to avoid being thrown in the games, bit his opponent's hand.

He released his grip, shouting: "You bite like a dog, Alcibiades!"

"No!" Alcibiades answered, "like a lion."

Other texts follow the Olympic ones—not only in Greek, but in Hebrew and Latin as well: funeral dirges and raucous jokes, curses, love songs, and beautiful prayers. Sometimes the passages are too hard for Jean François. Other ideas he understands despite his youth.

These are the great events in his life. Each passage is as much of a turning point for Jean François as Napoleon's early battles were revelations for him. Young Champollion's events are inward, not part of the great clamor and noise of the world. They take the boy away from the world.

He starts to write, copying many sayings in his notebooks. The pages are covered with laborious print, the round letters of a boy whose immature hand contrasts strangely with the meaning of the wide-ranging passages . . .

Watching a storm destroy his fleet, the Persian king Xerxes ordered that his soldiers whip the ocean.

It is an astonishing scene: the raging king at the edge of the dark water, the terrified soldiers whipping the high waves, the drowned sailors and shattered ships washing ashore. Jean François marvels at the strangeness of the world, its madness-in-meaning and meaning-in-madness! How far away is Xerxes and his rage from the narrow streets of Figeac; distant not only in time and place and feeling but in sound. Jean François first hears the story in Greek, beautiful inflections written in mysterious letters which only his brother can understand, or so it seems to him.

But other passages capture Jean François' imagination as
well, moments as ephemeral as a spider's web—
The sound of Roman laughter—

Who wants to make some ready money?
I'd be happy to.
Good, all you have to do is be crucified in my place!

A sudden realization, uttered in the midst of suffering—

We who see only one part of things, for us evil is evil. But to
God who understands all, evil is good.

An insult hurled at a man who has long since returned
to dust—

Your dirty legs are like a slave's.

Ancient epitaphs and wills and funeral orations, which,
unlike their solemn modern counterparts, laugh at human
frailty and greed—

All beneficiaries of my will inherit under this proviso: that
they cut my body in pieces and eat it with the townspeople
watching.

And all kinds of stories, portraits of lives that become more real for Jean François than the one he is living.

The desperate courage of a slave boy who dares to plead before the ruler of the world:

> The Emperor Augustus was dining with Vedius Pollio. One of the slave boys broke a crystal dish and Vedius ordered him to be thrown to the great lampreys in his fish pond. The boy tore himself away and fell at the Emperor's feet to ask him this only—that he should die some other way and not be fed to the fish. The indignant Emperor ordered the slave to be freed, that all Vedius' crystal dishes be smashed, and that the fish pond be filled up . . .

And miraculous stories—Zeus descending in a shower of gold and Venus rising from the sea. Hebrew miracles as well, stories told in a language as different from Greek, and reflecting a consciousness as far from the Olympian spirit as it is possible to be; tales of lepers raised from their dung heap to silken tents and goblets of gold—

> Four lepers sat outside the besieged city and said to one another: "Why should we wait here until we die? If we say: Let us enter the city, the famine is in the city, and we will die there. If we remain here, we will also die. Come and let us go over to the Aramean camp. If they spare our lives, we will live.

And if they kill us, we will simply die." But when they came to the Aramean camp, behold not a man was there . . . in great confusion and fear which the Lord had put in their breasts, the Arameans had fled at the sound of a driven leaf. They entered a tent, ate and drank, and took from there silver, gold, and clothing, and went and hid them. Then they returned and entered another tent, took from there also and went and hid them . . . Then they said: "We are not doing right. This day is a day of good tidings. Come, let us go and tell the king's household . . ."

And along with such stories as these, Jacques, who teaches his brother with opposing texts, also gives Jean François Roman "miracles" that mock all virtue, all belief:

. . . the governor of Ephesus sentenced a thief to be crucified . . . Night came and a soldier remained to prevent his relatives from taking down the body. Now as the soldier stood guard, he noticed a light shining in the caves nearby. Curious, he made his way there, stopping short at the sight of a beautiful woman so faithful, so pure that she had followed her husband's corpse to its tomb, determined to die by his side.

The soldier began to talk and the woman listened . . . and soon the doors of the tomb were closed upon them while he enjoyed her beauty . . . But the next morning when he emerged, he beheld a terrible sight: The cross was empty—

someone had taken down the thief's body in the night and buried it. Now he himself had the death penalty before him and, trembling, he ran to tell the woman. "The gods forbid," she cried out. "I would rather hang my dead husband on the cross than lose you . . ." Thus that day the townspeople were left to wonder at a miracle: how a dead man had climbed up onto the cross . . .

And the boy takes in everything, assimilates everything, making it his own; the gossip of the ancient world—

To the eunuch Bagoas, begging him to give him access to the fair one committed to his charge: "Thou, Bagoas, who art entrusted with the task of guarding thy mistress—I have but a couple of words to say to you, but they are weighty ones. Yesterday I saw a lady walking in the portico beneath the temple of Apollo . . .

Its precepts—

Learn the pleasure of despising pleasure.

A man keeps and feeds a lion. The lion owns a man.

If, as they say, I am only an ignorant man trying to be a philosopher, then that may be what a philosopher is.

Its virtue and its vice—its grandeur forms him.

Walk with swift feet, mortal, as you fulfill your uncertain destiny.

Intellectually, Jean François has begun to fall in love.

Bring water, bring wine, slave! Bring us crowns of flowers;
bring them so I may box with Eros.

The simplest question by Jean François is answered with
an outpouring of ardor from Jacques for whom the lessons
are a relief and a distraction. For a long time now Jacques
has been leading a severe existence. Every sou he has
earned has gone to support his parents in Figeac; and every
moment he can snatch from his drudgery has been used for
his studies.

With an iron discipline, he has taught himself Hebrew
and Latin and Greek, studying an enormous range of
ancient works; poring over them until finally his knowledge surpasses those with years of formal training.

Perhaps it is because his struggle has been so solitary, his
achievement so hidden, that Jacques takes his rejection so
much to heart. For without telling any one, he had applied
to join the scholars General Bonaparte is recruiting for an
extraordinary expedition. Going where? *Far from France.*
Lasting how long? *Six months or six years.* Everything about

it is shrouded in mystery, except the fact that Napoleon has gathered the best minds in his service.

There have been months of preparation, months of hope for Jacques, but now word has spread throughout the land: Bonaparte has suddenly slipped away in the middle of the night with his chosen scholars and his soldiers. Without a word of warning, he leaves Jacques Champollion, self-taught classicist and shipping clerk, at home.

And so Jacques throws himself into teaching his brother. He sets him riddles—

Why is the Chorus made up of old men in the first part of the Oresteia, *why of slave women in the second, why of the Furies in the third? What is the secret?*

He explains the subtle nature of language to him, how the dry rules of grammar can create a deep puzzle, choosing lines from the tragedies that turn in on themselves—

The living are killing the dead.
The dead are killing the living.

—in Greek a single phrase which expresses both meanings at once, the words themselves intertwining, as inseparable as the crimes of the past and present to which they refer.

More gifted than his hard-working brother, Jean François is able to remember long phrases and grasp difficult grammatical concepts after hearing them just once, astonishing Jacques with his facility. What his older brother has taken endless pains to learn, Jean François picks up with ease. He is a prodigy, Jacques quickly sees. When the older brother returns to Grenoble, he makes further sacrifices and finds the money for Jean François to be enrolled in school.

But if Jean François is an *enfant prodigue,* he is a temperamental one. He hates the discipline of his new school. He gets into fights with the other boys there every day. He becomes lazy and refuses to study anything. His head is filled with scenes from antiquity. Called upon to divide ten by two, to know the population of Figeac, to jump over a low hurdle, to spell his own name, he cannot.

Letters go back and forth between Grenoble and Figeac, between Jacques and Jean François, who appeals to his brother to let him live with him in Grenoble.

His brother answers, "If you want to come and live with me, you must study. An ignorant person can achieve nothing."

The boy says he cannot study what does not interest him: It has no meaning for him. What he does care about, he devours, obsessed. He begins to see that the world was old even in the first centuries, with exhausted oracles and gods who have ceased to speak.

He becomes preoccupied with time, with first beginnings, an endlessly receding horizon. *And before that? And before that?* he asks his brother like a child—relentlessly—but also like a philosopher. And with these insistent questions, he begins to stumble upon his fate, the life's work that will one day be his.

And before Christ?

The gods of Olympus, serene in beauty and power.

And before them?

Brutal monsters, the Titans—giants who howl with fear and rage as they devour their young.

And before that?

The earth and sky which for the Greeks always existed—but which the Hebrew God created from nothingness, from a single word, *Yehee!, Let there be!,* uttered in the darkness of endless night.

But still there is something *before that, before the Greeks and Hebrews,* something prior, preceding and half-forgotten like a dream or an hallucination: There is Egypt. Working his way back through the many moments in Egyptian time, first Arab, then Christian, Roman, Greek, Persian Egypt, Jean François arrives at the Egypt of the Pharaohs, dynasty after dynasty of rulers whose glory and splendor dazzled the world for millennia (the Old, Middle, and New Kingdoms) before beginning to wane one thousand years before

Christ. For when Athens was just a patch of rock-strewn ground and Jerusalem a crude Jebusite fortress; when Rome was a forest haunted by wolves, great pyramids and temples had already risen on the banks of the Nile.

The monuments, perfect in form and massive in size, are a measure of Egypt's power. And the inscriptions with which they are covered are a measure of her wisdom: the writing which the Greeks call hieroglyphs, holy carvings, and which the Egyptians call "the words of the gods." Fantastic pictures of walking jars and beasts with human bodies, a jumble of drawings: humpbacked vultures, squatting children, flowers and fruits, stars and palm trees and bald-headed priests, women giving birth, and male members spilling seed or urinating.

But what can they mean, these "words of the gods"? Their significance has been forgotten in the long course of time. "Speeches from the grave," the hieroglyphs will be called even in Roman times when there are still a few old priests who understand them. "The language of the dead," the Emperor Hadrian shrugs in the first century AD. But between "dying" and "dead" two centuries still remain and it is not until AD 394 that hieroglyphic writing, in use for more than three thousand years, is inscribed on a temple wall for the last time. And then silence descends: For fifteen hundred years the strange symbols stand as a puzzle and a challenge to all who see them. The cumulative experience and wisdom of a great civilization, they are a legacy—but only for the scholar wise enough to read them.

The young Jean François takes in the challenge, not yet seeing its connection to himself. This is the first moment of a great passion: The lover sees his beloved for the first time, but he does not yet understand his agitation. He sees the beloved and stands still in awe. There is no movement toward her, no declaration, no vow—no, the determined cry *I will decipher the hieroglyphs!* will come later. Jean François will not wait long, a few years, not more. When he is eleven he will take that step, too. For everything in his life takes place early, quickly, as if he knows that he has much to do in a short time. *A bow that is tightly strung must be unstrung by midday* will be one of his favorite quotations— from a pharaoh who also knew that he would not have many years to complete his desired tasks.

For the time being, though, it is enough that Jean François sees Egypt—and that he hears Egypt's mysterious silence of fifteen hundred years. Aware of the challenge, he turns to other projects, work for which his immature skills are more suitable. His brother's letters encourage him, exhort him not to be idle. He compiles a list of ancient peoples and then, still dwelling on origins, he compiles another list of famous dogs going back to the beginning of time. There is the dog of Odysseus and the dogs who devour the body of Jezebel and the "cynotherapists," the dogs of the healing temples, the Asklepieions, who gently walk or lay among the afflicted . . .

Thusor of Hermione, a blind boy, had his eyes licked by one of the Temple dogs and departed cured . . .

Thus, for Jean François the next years will be spent in study. In due course, his brother—finally!—will let him come to live with him in Grenoble although he never fulfills his brother's requirements of ". . . first learning the simple, the necessary facts and practical skills—not the least of which is to write legibly!"

From the narrow winding streets of Figeac, Jean François will be transported to a city two hundred miles away in which the snow-capped mountains can be seen on all sides. He will never see his mother again. She will die while he is learning Hebrew and Arabic and Chaldean, as well as Latin and Greek. For two years his brother will tutor him and then the next stage in his education will begin: the *lycée*.

Two contrary elements will be present from this time on. Two sign posts as contrary as east and west mark his way: *the inevitable* and *the improbable*.

For what could be more improbable than the fate awaiting him? What could be more far-fetched—who would have guessed it?—that a young boy living in a small French town would conceive a passion such as the one which consumes Jean François? Who could have known that the strange carvings covering the tombs and temples of Egypt—mere chicken scratchings to a philistine mind!—would make everything else pale in the life of Jean François?

But if it is a strange, a fantastic passion, it is also, like all great passions, an inevitable one. To understand this inevitability, though, to see how it came about, one must ignore external circumstances. The logic of Jean François' development is an inner one. To understand, to be in sympathy with him, one must ask along with this young French boy—and with the same naïve wonder—*And before that? And before that? And even before that?* until one is standing in blinding light before a silent Egyptian tomb.

Chapter Three

The Promised Land

WHILE CHAMPOLLION SITS at his lessons, another boy, a British "boy," appears on a London stage—eighteen-year-old Mademoiselle Legrini, the sensation of the day. Hair cropped short, she wears a schoolboy's cap and tight breeches, and she saunters across the stage with a sexy swagger, singing a bawdy song while showing off her famous legs. Her fans go wild. Among them is Napoleon's chief opponent in Europe, the pleasure-loving, corpulent Prince Regent. He rules England during the times when his father is mad. And though no warrior, he is one of the best dancers in the land.

On her way back to her dressing room, Legrini passes an Italian compatriot. She and the strongman Belzoni are both main attractions of the day. Their acts, her singing and his feats of strength, are part of a gala performance occasioned by the war with France which any day might be fought on English soil. Or, as a patriotic poster in front of the theater proclaims:

This day was published,
An
Address to the People
of the United Kingdom of
Great Britain and Ireland,
on the threatened
INVASION.

Among the inexpressibly dreadful consequences which are sure to attend the conquest of your Island by the French, there is one of so horrible a nature as to deserve distinct notice. This barbarous, but most artful people, when first they invade a country in the conquest of which they apprehend any difficulty, in order to obtain the confidence of the people, compel their troops to observe the strictest discipline, and often put a soldier to death for stealing the most trifling article. Like spiders they artfully weave a web round their victim, before they begin to prey upon it. But when their success is complete then let loose their troops, with resistless fury, to commit the most horrible excesses, and to pillage, burn, and desolate without mercy and without distinction. But the practice to which I particularly allude will make your blood freeze in your veins . . .

And so on. The details, a mixture of truth and propaganda, are calculated to arouse fear and indignation. Crowds gather to read the poster, jostling one another beside a man hawking plaster casts of Mademoiselle Legrini's famous legs (the proceeds also going for the cause!)—"*La jambe de Legrini*," the leg of Legrini, described by reviewers as being ". . . so beautiful, of such a symmetry, a *moelleux* and a play of muscle that the sight of it will enchant any lover of art!"

The audience agrees, for long after Mademoiselle Legrini has finished, the cries for her to return do not die down . . . until the giant Belzoni steps out onto the stage. He is handsome, with a long auburn beard flowing over his broad chest. And he is enormous. Six foot six with rippling muscles, his huge figure dwarfs the ten large men already in place. They stand center stage on a metal frame to which a harness is attached. The strongman crouches down, slips the harness over his shoulders and then slowly lifts the staggering weight. The audience, after a stunned silence, breaks into an ecstatic roar.

The applause lasts so long, in fact, that most performers would find the act a difficult one to follow. But the young girl waiting backstage has no qualms—having been dead for more than two thousand years, according to the doctor who has brought her mummy from Egypt and who claims that he can understand the inscriptions on her coffin, those bare-breasted goddesses and the jackal-headed gods.

The curtain is lowered and the learned doctor steps in front. He begins his introductory patter while the mummy is wheeled into place: "An ancient princess will be unwrapped tonight for the benefit of Science and for your personal edification! A girl who died tragically young, as inscriptions on her coffin indicate."

Backstage Belzoni pauses at the sight of the mummified princess. The handsome, laughing strongman crouches down, kneeling by her side. He has no idea that one day he will be surrounded by thousands of mummies, both human and animal—cats and crocodiles and bulls that were, for the Egyptians, divine. Nor does Belzoni dream that he will almost become a mummy himself as he crawls through the underground labyrinths of the City of the Dead, bats in flight extinguishing his torch, leaving him lost in dark winding tunnels, choking on the dust of the disintegrating and once sacred flesh. He will travel throughout the ancient land, be overwhelmed by Ramesses' fantastic colossi, witness the lonely splendor of Abu Simbel. This colossus showman will explore the burial chambers of the Shining and Beautiful Pyramid, the Pyramid which is Pure of Places, the Pyramid where the Ba-spirit Rises. And his name will be forever linked with Egypt when he discovers her most famous temples and long-forgotten tombs.

But at this juncture, the corpse of the young-yet-ancient princess is just a rival act. He is a sensation—a Seven Days' Wonder—and so is she. As the curtain rises, to peals of laughter he gives her a kiss before being shooed from the stage.

It is a theatrical gesture, obscene and unforgettable, *Grand Guignol* and nothing more. For Belzoni is a showman through and through who has used his strength to escape the poverty into which he was born. As a boy of twelve he was left to make his way in the world, but now he has begun to use his mind as well. It is a creative mind; the strongman is studious and imaginative. He gives himself no rest after his performances are over: working, inventing, experimenting into the small hours of the night, struggling to discover the necessary *something,* the undreamed of *whatever* that will complete his transformation from a boy sleeping in alleys and fighting for scraps thrown in the street to a man of the world who has achieved fortune and fame.

And when he finally does create an invention that seems promising—a hydraulic irrigation wheel more powerful than anything tried before—it will be this practical feat of engineering that will bring him to Egypt, a land that depends on the waters of the Nile.

But Belzoni's hydraulic wheel will ultimately fail and be forgotten. Yet in those desert wastes, among colossal statues and ancient tombs, the strongman, a colossus himself, will put his enormous energy and stamina to good use. He will return to Europe with his undreamed-of wonders: sixty-three-foot-tall statues of pharaohs and soaring obelisks and alabaster sarcophagi. Covered with inscriptions, these monuments will ultimately be essential to Champollion's work.

For the time being, though, Belzoni is as indifferent to Egypt as the princess he has just kissed is to him: "She did not shudder at my embrace!" he jokes to a writer for the broadsheets, a gossip from the *Gentleman's Review* who dawdles backstage, knowing the strongman is always good for a quote. The two men stand together, talking and laughing in the wings, watching as the princess' body is exposed layer by layer. Exotic flutes trill in the background, accompanying *oohs* and *aahs* as scraps of parchment, ancient spells, and strange amulets are found hidden in the bandages. And the phony doctor is also stripped naked onstage: stripped of his learned pretensions. For the coffin inscriptions, hieroglyphs he claims to have read, he cannot have understood. The mummy has—*or once had*—a male member.

This fact is not immediately known. By an ancient saving grace (saving for the doctor), this masculine member was removed and embalmed separately in imitation of Osiris, god of the dead, who is murdered and castrated by his brother—and revived and made whole by the magic of his sister-wife Isis. For in the primal world of the Egyptian gods nothing is obscene, the facts of the body are interwoven with the soul in tales childlike both in their violence and their innocence.

A real doctor, a serious young man named Thomas Young who has been granted his degree not by theatrical courtesy but by Emmanuel College, Cambridge, comes backstage to examine the mummy. An aristocrat and an intellectual with wide-ranging interests, Young will be drawn to the riddle of the hieroglyphs not, like Champollion, for metaphysical reasons but because of the logical puzzle it presents. Although a good classical scholar, he will never match the vast linguistic resources Champollion acquires. He will never know Coptic or Persian or Chaldean or immerse himself in Egyptian history and geography so that thousands of ancient place-names are on the tip of his tongue. This limitation will determine Young's *mathematical* approach when he takes up the problem in the course of time.

At the present, however, Young determines the "princess'" sex right away. And more besides: He finds among the linen wrappings fragments of a poem written in Greek on gazelle skin, a scrap of leather used like old newspaper to wrap fish. Perhaps this had been thrust between the toes to keep them apart or perhaps it had been tucked in as padding for this long-dead man's heels.

The Greek on the scrap dates the mummy as being late in Egyptian history, sometime after Alexander conquers

Egypt in 330 BC when both the Greek and Egyptian languages are in use. And thus the serious young scholar,
unable to read the hieroglyphs on the coffin, can read the
ancient dialogue written on the hide of a gazelle.

The poem describes a scene between a girl and her
would-be lover. With many lines crumbled into dust, it is
like a conversation overheard from the past, words and half
phrases carried on the winds of time—

> . . . *simply restrain yourself* . . .
> *or if you can't, there, in our house, is a girl*
>
> *. . .*
>
> *why then grieve her?*
>
> *This was her plea. So I formally answered:*
>
> *"There are many sweet gifts for young men from the goddess,*
> *Pleasures that stop at the brink*
> *One will suffice.*
>
> *If the god wills,*
> *. . . pour my libation*
> *Out at your grassy gateway . . .*
> *Do not deny me the threshold, beloved . . .*
> *I'll not break in . . .*
> *As for Neoboule, she is for others.*
> *Let who will have her*
> *She is full blown and her grace is gone.*

. . .

. . .

I prefer you."

This said, I laid the girl down among the flowers in my
soft cloak.
I embraced her gently.
I touched her flesh with my hands.
She remained still but she trembled like a fawn as I
released the white force of my passion.

A fitting poem for Young to find curled beneath the
"princess'" leg: a warning at the beginning of his career.
For like the *demivierge,* the half-virgin who both accepts
and refuses her importunate lover, Egypt will never give
herself completely to Champollion or to Young, to Bonaparte and his scholars, or to those who come after. She will
forever remain a mystery, half-revealed and half-hidden
beneath her eternally shifting sand.

囗 囗 囗

THE MOON SHINES down on a fleet sailing across the Mediterranean. The deck of the flagship is brightly lit with torches burning around a raised platform. A play is in progress, not a bawdy comedy like the ones which have pleased the soldiers and sailors on other nights, but a dramatic adaptation of Goethe's novella, *The Sorrows of Young Werther.*

It is a strange choice for the night's entertainment, but the men are now used to their general's unpredictable ways. At the same time he is both the perfect soldier and completely unsoldierly. Napoleon has filled valuable space, they whisper, storage room another general would use for ammunition and provisions, with box after box of scientific instruments; with printing presses, presses set up with Arabic and Greek as well as Roman type; and with a huge library of books that he has had taken on board besides. Reference and technical and historical works are stacked in crates beside the pawing and nervous horses, of which there are not enough—a fact that will force most of the light cavalry, when they reach Egypt, to march on foot.

But then if there are not enough horses, there are plenty of scholars: 167 of them, the general's "favorite mistress" as the men call them. Night after night, Bonaparte sits on deck debating, arguing, theorizing with them as the ships make their way through dangerous waters. The fleet is in a race with the stronger British Navy, England's most powerful weapon in its life-and-death struggle against revolutionary France.

And so, though all eyes are on the actors, everyone is aware that at any moment the British might suddenly materialize. In the unequal battle that would follow, General Bonaparte, his scholars, his books, printing presses, and scientific instruments would all be sent to the bottom of the sea: thirty-eight thousand men, including the soldier playing the tragic Werther, a burly dragoon (totally miscast!) who throws out his arms as he declaims: "Treat my heart as a sick child! Grant it whatever it requests!"

But the British do not interrupt the performance. Luck has been with Napoleon since the night the expedition left France when a terrific storm dispersed the British warships threatening Toulon. "An act of God!" the atheistic revolutionaries joke. As the British struggle to regroup, Napoleon's ships slip past them and out to the open sea. A fleet is sent from England to find the French fleet—but just where to look in the Mediterranean is the question: Sicily? Egypt? the Greek Isles?

Napoleon's saving grace is the secrecy in which he has cloaked the expedition. The secretary of the navy himself did not know its destination until hours before the departure. In fact, at first a completely different scheme had been planned: All along France's coast preparations had been made for an invasion of Britain, a direct assault across the Channel which was to have been launched that spring. Though this plan is abandoned, the preparations are kept up as a smokescreen.

Such an invasion would have been in line with Napoleon's boldness. There is nothing the young general shrinks from: He will cross the Alps with an army on sleds and pack donkeys, he will attack when he is outnumbered and outflanked, he will gamble and win time and again when the odds are against him. However, at least at this stage in his career, his boldness is tempered by a keen appreciation of military realities.

An invasion across the Channel would fail. "The way to strike at England is through Egypt," he lectures the Directors of France (lawyers and an ex-Abbé with little military experience), unfolding a global strategy in which British trade routes are cut off, the British hold on India is destroyed, Britain is isolated, then defeated.

"And the nation that defeats Britain could rule the world!" he continues with a wildness that makes the Directors wonder if he is mad: "After Egypt, I shall march upon Damascus and Aleppo, increasing my army as I go . . . for I shall announce to the people the overthrow of the tyrannous pashas. Then with overwhelming forces, I shall take

Constantinople [Istanbul], making an end of Turkey, and found a new and great empire. This will bring me immortal fame. Perhaps I shall then make my way home through Adrianople or Vienna, after annihilating the House of Hapsburg."

The five sober Directors are right to wonder. There is, of course, more than a little madness, grandiosity, and megalomania in Napoleon's plan: "I am the instrument of Providence. She will use me as long as I accomplish her designs, then she will break me!" He rants on, talking of cutting a canal through the Isthmus of Suez in the place where the ancient one of the pharaohs had been, describing a hundred fantastic projects from curing Egypt's plague-ridden people to improving its beer!—all the while he urges the hesitating lawyers not to delay: "You do what you have to do and do it quickly. Be ruthless about it!"

They know that this inspired soldier means what he says, for hadn't he saved the Directory in its early days by turning cannon on the demonstrating crowds, leaving a broad swathe of men and women lying dead in the streets? "A whiff of grapeshot," he muses afterward, "would have saved the King . . ."

But if Napoleon is mad and in his madness capable of anything, there is an eminently sane man listening to him along with the Directors. Foreign Minister Talleyrand agrees with the general, at least as far as Egypt is concerned.

As for the rest—the world—"There is time," Talleyrand shrugs in his discreet and diplomatic way.

Talleyrand is an uncompromising realist and will never really understand Napoleon's worldview. He is a wily aristocrat who flees the revolution at just the right time and returns at the correct moment as well. A handsome, cultured man of forty, with catlike agility and elegant manners, he always lands on his feet.

For him, glory is a word for schoolboys. The conquest of Egypt is a practical step, an expedient démarche and nothing more. But Napoleon, like Alexander the Great, goes to Egypt to find out if he is a god. The general wants to be an immortal, to have immortal fame. And the painters, sculptors, poets, playwrights he commissions at every turn, the boatsful of scholars he takes with him are all part of this quest.

"The true conquests, those that will never be forgotten are those that are wrested from ignorance!" Napoleon declares, a statement crucial to understanding the philosopher-soldier that he is. With scholars in tow, he claims Egypt in the name of knowledge. It is his plan to study everything about this forgotten land, its flora and fauna, its birds, its fish, and even its insects, to understand its diseases, to chart its deserts and to sketch its crumbling antiquities in order to enlarge mankind's knowledge of itself.

"In Egypt, at the crossroads of Asia, Europe, and Africa, knowledge flourished at the dawn of time," one of the savants writes later on, describing the feeling of his colleagues for the country. "Here Homer, Lycurgus, Solon, Pythagoras, and Plato came to learn the sciences, religion, and the laws."

As much as the present, it is this past of Egypt that Napoleon wants for his own. From the moment he reaches her shores, he will struggle like a man possessed to obtain it. If a languor descends on his soldiers who suffer from the unbearable heat, he urges them on, sets them a thousand tasks to perform when they are not fighting, hitches them to the guns during forced marches when their animals drop in exhaustion. Napoleon himself holds men in his arms in the pesthouse who are dying of plague; the moment becomes a famous painting. Napoleon is looking up, he is always looking up in the paintings as if communing with the gods, indifferent to danger, in love with fate.

"The sciences are the glory of the human mind, the arts bequeath noble deeds to our offspring," proclaims this creator of academies on warships, this greatest lawgiver since Justinian, and this god who will practice any bloodshed or brutality he pleases. Are not gods above the law? Thousands of prisoners will be slaughtered during the eastern campaign since he does not have enough food to feed them. At the suggestion of freeing them, he goes into a rage. "Free them?" He shakes his fist at an appalled officer who opposes him. "If that's the way you feel, go, hide away in a monastery and never come out!"

Bloodstained, godlike, cruel, artistic, philosophic, and immoral, he proclaims, "The French people would rather win a great mathematician, painter, or other man of note than win the wealthiest of provinces." He makes this boast not knowing that Fate is listening and will take him at his word. For if he will have an intellectual triumph in Egypt—page after page of the twenty-three volume *Description of Egypt* is edited in his own hand—it will come with a crushing military defeat: the first in his career.

This is still in the future. The present finds him haranguing the stolid lawyers (and one ex-Abbé!) of the Directory, hurling phrases at them in his passionate and irresistible way—though they try to resist. They listen and they doubt.

For they are practical men who recoil from this wild-eyed fanatic with his long hair and his scraggly looks, his pallor, his weary eyes and visionary speeches whose every other word is *glory* and *might*. It is Talleyrand who wins the day by making a few reasonable observations, pointing out that such a scheme had been contemplated since the time of Louis XIV—only there had always been one difficulty or another in the past.

Reassuringly, the handsome Talleyrand is a man who cares more for pleasure than for glory, and more for money than either. Throughout his career, he demands huge bribes—whether he is foreign minister during the Directory, or under Napoleon, or after Napoleon, too (for he will last and last and last).

He always gets the fabulous sums he requires, for his recommendation carries weight—as it does now when he agrees with Napoleon that Egypt is ripe. What does it matter that the country belongs to the Ottoman Empire whose sultan is an ally of France? Such trifles can be left to the diplomats while Napoleon wins the war.

A deal is struck: Talleyrand himself will go to Istanbul to negotiate—though once Napoleon has left for Egypt, the Foreign Minister stays comfortably at home. He understands that what the Directors really want is to get Napoleon out of the way. The popular young hero is a threat to their power. Let the sultan send troops to crush the arrogant madman! Let him return defeated. Better yet, let him fall in battle on the desert sands.

Bonaparte's victories have made him overbearing. Has the revolution been won for such a brute to rule France? Thus, the Directors whisper among themselves, taking dark counsel with their Foreign Minister. Publicly, though, they praise Napoleon, and none with more feeling than the soft-spoken Talleyrand:

"All France will be free—with only the exception of Napoleon. That is his destiny . . . To carry the burdens of

France . . ." Such is Talleyrand's style: eloquent and insincere. One day, in a rage over his treachery and betrayal, Napoleon will call Talleyrand *Shit in a silk stocking!*

For the time being the two are friends. Talleyrand embraces Napoleon on the eve of his departure. With a soft kiss of Judas, he speeds him on his way.

口 口 口

THIRTY-EIGHT THOUSAND men—the Army of the Orient as Napoleon calls it—leave France, together with one woman. Pauline Fourès, a newly married lieutenant's wife, cuts off her long blond hair, straps on a breast-flattener borrowed from nuns and pretends to have been a drummer boy in the Italian war. In the chaos onboard she can easily wander to and fro without attracting much attention—as can a Bourbon spy named D'Entraigues, a follower of the beheaded Louis and of his gouty brother, also Louis (the XVIII), the so-called "legitimate" ruler of France, who sits spinning webs in exile in London.

The soldiers leave France on a fleet of four hundred transports with an escort of thirteen heavily armed ships of the line and seven frigates, easily maneuverable craft. The boats carry seventy-five siege guns and mortars, ninety field guns, 1230 horses and leave from five ports of embarkment to rendezvous at sea.

And though the men of war are impressive, the transports onto which the soldiers are crowded are a motley collection of merchant vessels, fishing boats, and pleasure boats pressed into service at the last moment. Whatever floats will do.

It is a fighting force assembled with remarkable speed as well as secrecy, a feat achieved through the energy of one man: Napoleon. The impatient general has given the near bankrupt Directors of France no peace: *Money and men* is his constant cry. He has even gone back and ruthlessly plundered a second time all the provinces he has snatched from Austria and added to France. "The Hapsburg Empire," he shouts contemptuously at the defeated Emperor's envoy, "is an old serving woman used to being raped!"

Millions of francs are stolen from the "liberated" Italian territories and a forced "loan" is arranged from the Pope and from the new Helvetic (Swiss) Republic as well. Thousands of men are recruited for service all along the coast, and dishonest contractors are threatened with drastic punishment for delays. These same dishonest contractors are lining the pockets of Napoleon's new wife and the lover she has already taken, a dandy named Hippolyte Charles.

With curled hair and a wardrobe of all the latest fashions, he has won Josephine's heart. And the two are war speculators as well as lovers.

Charles, with his elegance and his cynical witticisms, is more pleasing to Josephine than the earnest and romantic Napoleon. During her months in the shadow of the guillotine, she vowed that if she survived, she would live for pleasure, a vow that she has begun to fulfill.

A month before Napoleon's departure, the affair almost comes to light. A maid, dismissed by Josephine, vengefully tells Napoleon everything. Josephine denies the charges and her husband believes her because he wants to. He pays her debts, he sends her jewels and ardent letters, he takes her children for his own, enrolling her daughter in an expensive school and arranging for her son (who is only a few years younger than her new lover) to accompany him to Egypt. Napoleon would have taken her to Egypt as well, but a balcony collapsed under her and she has been confined to bed for months. She means everything to him. But at this stage for the sensual Creole with her memories and her many lovers, her marriage to the lovesick soldier is a financial arrangement, nothing more.

"I embrace every part of you, my vulture," he muses in a never-sent letter, "but are you faithful to me?"

Another farce, not a domestic one, is quickly to follow. For the expedition's first port of call is Malta, an island in the Mediterranean that has been ruled by a medieval crusading order, the Knights of St. John of Jerusalem, for almost three hundred years.

Under the protection of the tsar, headed by a German grand master, the knights tyrannize the island's native population. They have long since ceased to do any fighting themselves. The thousand cannon on its massive battlements are unused and rusty. And the ten-foot-thick fortress walls mean nothing. The gates are quickly opened by corrupt knights Napoleon has taken care to bribe.

Fearful of the pursuing British, Napoleon quickly takes what he has come for. Chest after chest of treasure is carried out from vaults under the order's church. The grand master is banished, a small force is left to rule in the name of France and the expedition to Egypt is once again on its way.

What is the nature of this land to which we are going? is a topic Napoleon proposes to his scholars (at least those who are not belowdeck with seasickness) for that night's debate.

And when that is finished, another question: *Is there life on other planets?* And another: *Is there any truth in premonitions?*

Finally, as the wine flows and tongues loosen, the question: *Is there God?*

Question: Are the people of the Egypt more sensual than others? "A beautiful woman who dies is not given to the embalmers in Egypt," says Herodotus, "until her body has begun to decay . . ."

Question follows question as in the mist and the dark, the British Fleet passes the French, barely seventy miles away.

口 口 口

THE EGYPT TOWARD which Napoleon and his fleet are sailing is a land ruled by slaves.

As children they have been taken by force from remote villages in the Caucasus and raised by the Turks for one purpose and one purpose only: war.

With no past and no future—they may never marry or have children—they are trained night and day how to live on horseback, to wield their magnificent jeweled scimitars, to look death in the face without flinching; and while riding at full gallop, to bend down and, with one stroke, decapitate a bull held in place by their teacher. Such is their instruction in the art of war.

Coats of chain mail under their robes, gilded helmets on their heads, armed to the teeth with battle axes and daggers, spears, sabers, lances, and three sets of pistols, carrying all their worldly wealth in saddle bags beneath them—

another reason not to let themselves be taken alive—they charge with the speed of lightning on Arabian mounts as they shout blood-curdling cries. These were the warriors—called Mamelukes, "owned men"—that Napoleon had come to conquer with his newly impressed recruits.

He begins his assault while still far away at sea, devising one edict after another to win the people over to him from their rulers, making good use of the Arabic printing presses he has brought along. The Mamelukes have been selfish and tyrannical rulers. Twenty-three Mameluke "beys" or warlords continually fight among themselves for power, causing devastation and ruin in the land. And though the ethereal beauty of the tombs and mosques they create will be lasting tributes to their glory, truly poetry in stone, the people hate them for their cruelty and greed.

Too long have the Mamelukes ruled Egypt! The hour of their destruction has arrived!

Napoleon announces in the first of his pamphlets,

Too long has this horde of slaves tyrannized over you, oh people of the Nile! You will be told that I come to destroy your religion. Do not believe it. I come to restore your rights and punish the usurpers! For I venerate God and his prophet and the holy Koran!

All men are equal before God; but it is wisdom, talents and virtues that make differences between men. Now what wisdom, what talents, what virtues distinguish the Mamelukes that they should possess all that is sweet in life? Is there a beautiful estate? It belongs to the Mamelukes. Is there a beautiful horse, a beautiful house? They belong to the Mamelukes. There formerly existed in Egypt great cities, great canals, great commerce; by what means have they been destroyed if not by the Mamelukes?

There is much truth in what he says, though it is also skillful propaganda. Egypt is sunk in centuries of lethargy and oppression. The French will encounter a world that is still medieval, its population poor and diseased and superstitious, their lives barely rising above those of their beasts.

It is not only the French fleet but the modern world approaching Egypt while the bejeweled slaves ride furiously to and fro in the desert, their shouts echoing in their schools of war.

Question: How to bring the ideals of the revolution to Egypt? How to bring energy and activity to this stagnating land?

Question: What is the best manner to construct ovens? How can justice and education be improved in accordance with the wishes of the people? Question: How is it possible to purify the waters of the Nile?

Chapter Four

Two Beginnings

Cairo. 1824, a quarter of a century
after Napoleon invades—and then abandons—Egypt.

A YOUNG MAN walks with his father in a walled garden behind their house. They talk of many things: politics, religion, history. The father has seen much and his observations are illuminating.

But as the old man reminisces, assassins appear beneath the dusty palms and towering cypresses. They are so swift that the young man does not even have time to cry out before they slit his throat. He falls to the ground, dying amid lush foliage while the murderers turn back to search the house, pushing the old man aside.

The house is pillaged—not of its gold and silver but of

manuscripts. These writings have caused the tragedy, the works of the old man—the "most learned Jabarti"—who for the last fifty years has been recording the history of his native land. But while his *Chronicle of the French in Egypt* has won him fame, when he brings his history up to the year 1821, he makes the mistake of criticizing the current ruler, Mohammed Ali. He pays for it with the life of his son.

His life is spared, however, since Mohammed Ali admires his learning and the beauty of his prose. But it is a broken life. Withdrawing into his gloomy, medieval house, the historian gives up writing and spends his last years in grief and mourning.

In place of a son, Jabarti leaves behind his chronicle: an account that views Napoleon and his army not only on the battlefield, but from a thousand unthought-of angles—in whorehouses and barbershops, in cafés and in the bazaars. Jabarti records the endless Egyptian whisperings about the infidels. Even the immodest manner in which the foreign soldiers relieve themselves is not overlooked.

Jabarti is also scathing on the subject of the Mamelukes, scorning their cruelty, arrogance, and blindness to the approaching danger. If the Mamelukes think of the Europeans at all, they imagine a soft, pleasure-loving people, easily crushed "donkey boys." Against such weak enemies they have not bothered to take the most elementary precautions, leaving their harbors and coastline virtually undefended.

Ignorant not only of the psychology of the Europeans but of all modern developments in warfare, the Mamelukes put their complete trust in a whirlwind cavalry charge. This fearless charge depends, above all, on a collective indifference to death acquired through a lifetime of rigorous training. Their strength has nothing to do with individual acts of courage, with exceptional bravery or heroism rewarded with bits of ribbon and medals. No, if the Mameluke charge is undefeated, it is because thousands of phenomenally skilled swordsmen ride together as one man, a mystical doctrine of *fana,* or self-annihilation, imparting a wild joy to their savage cries.

Thus matters stand on the eve of the invasion when, Jabarti tells us, a fleet suddenly appears off the shore of Alexandria. First, ten heavily armed men of war, and then fifteen more linger on the horizon, just discernible to those in the city. An excited crowd gathers at the docks and watches. Finally, toward the end of the day, a skiff is lowered from one of the warships and heads toward the harbor.

Sitting regally among the rowing sailors is a young, one-armed officer in a uniform covered with gold braid and medals. He neither gives nor returns salutations as the skiff makes its way among the fishing boats and barges and the graceful *feluccas,* the light Egyptian craft that swiftly ply back and forth in the crowded harbor.

Even when the skiff reaches shore, the officer maintains

his self-contained stance, calmly stepping onto the dock as if the sudden appearance of a European war fleet is an everyday affair. Through an interpreter, he states that he is the British commander, Admiral Nelson. He asks to speak to the governor. And then in his matter-of-fact manner, without menace or swagger, he settles down to wait amid the bales of unloaded goods and the drying fish and the murmuring crowd.

Such calm is a British ideal: *nil admirari,* to be astonished at nothing. And certainly Nelson is a perfect representative of his class and nation. A clever, bold officer—implacable. The loss of an arm during fighting off the Spanish coast cost him a mere two weeks of active service, no more. Nelson is given command of this crucial mission despite his youth, the Admiralty choosing him for his total war philosophy. His goal in battle is not booty or ransom or even a formal victory according to the accepted rules of naval engagement. He is satisfied with nothing less than complete destruction of the enemy.

But Nelson has been overly eager in pursuit of "the Devil's child," as he calls Napoleon. Though he is quite correct in putting Egypt at the top of his list of Napoleon's possible destinations, he has made a mistake in timing. The British warships travel faster than the heavily laden French transports, with their thousands of men. Thus, without realizing it, Nelson overtook Napoleon's fleet in the middle of the Mediterranean, and arrived in Egypt three days ahead of him.

The governor comes to meet Nelson, with him a large retinue of officials and guards. It is a brilliant spectacle, the governor advancing down the wharf under a red silk canopy surrounded by turbaned courtiers and Nubian soldiers, armor glittering in the sun. And at the edge of the crowd, there is a sharp-eyed observer who records the exchange: the historian Jabarti whose writings later doom him.

The English told us that the French had set out from their country with a great fleet. They further said: "We are their enemies and do not know in which direction they intend to sail. Perhaps they will attack you suddenly and you will not be able to repel them."

However, al-Sayyid Kurayyim thought their words to be trickery.

The English leader requested: "Sell us water and provisions and we shall stay in our ships lying in wait for them."

Kurayyim replied: "We do not accept what you say nor will we give you anything."

Then he expelled the foreigners that God's will might be fulfilled.

One can read between the lines: Nelson, no diplomat, plays his hand badly. Unused to eastern circumlocution and stratagems, he states his business brusquely, tersely, like a soldier, and he is not believed.

The moment is decisive: If Nelson had stayed, Napoleon would never have been able to land. He and his army would have been destroyed on sight. "But God's will was otherwise," as Jabarti puts it. The setting sun shimmers over the Mediterranean, its deep blue waters streaked with green and turquoise swells. The muezzin's long, wailing calls to prayer echo from hundreds of mosques as the one-armed admiral is rowed back to his ships.

Nelson heads north, continuing his search off the coasts of Italy and Greece. Egypt is left to its fate.

ロ ロ ロ

ALL OF FRANCE follows the Egyptian campaign with bated breath, wildly celebrating Napoleon's victories with the enthusiasm of a people who have had their fill of revolution and terror and are eager now for glory.

Terrible disasters, one after another, quickly follow these

victories, but it does not matter for Napoleon turns them into "immortal triumphs" in the dispatches he sends home. Perhaps extravagances, lies, or boasts are better descriptions of the news Napoleon sends back of the Egyptian debacle.

Then suddenly he is back. One day, stirring military bulletins are everywhere: "The epoch-making French army has this month," etc., etc. The next day "The Sultan El-Kebir,"—the Great Sultan as the Egyptians call him—is seen at the Paris opera, barely acknowledging ecstatic applause before withdrawing to the back of his box with a mysterious, preoccupied air, indifferent to such displays or feigning indifference. As a careful reader of Machiavelli, Napoleon knows that the prince must make his presence rare. And it is a prince that he now wants to be, his new republican title "First Consul" notwithstanding.

Napoleon returns alone, a fact unremarked upon at the time. He had slipped out of Egypt secretly, at night, leaving the pitiable remnant of his army to await the final defeat by themselves.

Even General Kléber, the next in command, is informed of his departure after the fact. A letter from Napoleon is given to him beginning (in true princely style) "By the time you receive this, I will have left Egypt" and going on to instruct Kléber to "hold out for as long as possible."

And Kléber, scatologically cursing the day he ever set eyes on Napoleon, does hold out. For almost a year, he attempts to salvage what he can. Finally, he dies on a Cairo street, cut down by a religious fanatic who leaps out from amid a crowd of beggars and raises the cry which has echoed in Egypt from the moment the French arrive: "Death to the infidel dogs!" Josephine will name a pale, hundred-petaled rose in poor Kléber's honor.

Command is left to a lovestruck, struggling general called Menou. While the demoralized army Napoleon had abandoned, decimated by disease, disintegrates before Menou's eyes, and while Napoleon, in Paris, is fêted and applauded, the middle-aged Menou, swathed in white robes, publicly converts to Islam in the vast courtyard of the Ibn Tulun Mosque, where the French conquerors had stabled their horses when they first arrived.

"There is no God but God and Mohammed is his prophet!" the general declares in the presence of his broken, sorrowful officers, and before those of the savants who choose to attend. Perhaps this is a genuine profession of faith. Or perhaps it is a desperate political gesture, a last, futile attempt to gain popular support. Or perhaps it is neither of these but a case of violent, romantic passion overtaking a middle-aged man. Menou had fallen head-over-heels in love with a virtuous sixteen-year-old beauty who would not marry a Christian. In any case, this conversion does not save the situation: The French are forced to surrender.

The surrender is a long, drawn-out task, entailing much emotional back-and-forth and much senseless delay. By the time the surviving soldiers straggle back to France, by the time the appalling stories of what happened in Egypt become public knowledge, it no longer matters. Napoleon has, by then, seized power and, at the head of a new army, has gone on to achieve one victory after another.

With dazzling speed, Napoleon regains his Italian conquests, lost by the incompetent Directors while he was in Egypt, and achieves a decisive victory at Marengo that will lead the Austrians, the Prussians, and the Russians to sue for peace. The first coalition against France is vanquished.

Peace. Finally, there is a brief interval, a breathing space that lasts long enough for Napoleon to declare himself emperor before returning to his art. For he is an artist by nature, a temperamental, moody, passionate artist whose medium is war.

He is intractable. He is stubborn and provocative. Soon a second coalition against France must be defeated. But now it is as emperor that Napoleon leads the French armies to triumph—through Italy, Belgium, the German Kingdoms, the Austrian Empire, and finally the battle of Austerlitz, his masterpiece.

It is fought under a clear winter sky which becomes a catchphrase: *the cold sun of Austerlitz*. Indeed it can be taken as a metaphor for the stage in his career at which Napoleon has arrived. For unlike the Egyptian campaign—all furious heat, all willfulness and passion—by the time Napoleon fights at Austerlitz, he has achieved a balance between instinct and reason, boldness and prudence, passion and dispassion. He tempts the tsar to pursue the supposedly "retreating" French troops, drawing him into an untenable position. Then he surrounds the combined Russian-Prussian-Austrian force and cuts it to bits.

It is a brilliant piece of strategy conceived the night before when, sleepless and brooding, Napoleon makes the rounds of his troops, stalking back and forth on next-day's battlefield, giving his imagination, his intellect, his instincts free play.

Half-abstracted, distant, he stops every so often to scrutinize some insignificant detail: the slope of a small hillock, the buttons on a soldier's jacket. He mutters to himself or stares into the distance. Then he jokes with his soldiers—coarse jokes, talking obscenely of the "impatiently waiting" women of the enemy. He becomes eloquent about glory, practicing the genius he had for "getting others to die for him." Finally, he falls silent. Looking over the dark field, he comes up with the inspired plan which brings Russia to its knees a second time, along with Prussia and the haughty Austrian Empire. The second coalition against France is vanquished.

Thus Napoleon dazzles the world. On a raft in the

middle of the Nieman River, at a point equidistant from both army camps, Tsar Alexander publicly embraces the "usurper, the Corsican upstart," calling him "brother." The young and beautiful queen of Prussia—décolleté and shameless—outrageously flirts with him, trying to win favors for her defeated land. Princes and kings hang anxiously on his every word.

He has fulfilled his boast: the challenge he threw to the world at his coronation. At the height of the ceremony, Napoleon seizes the crown from the pope's hands and, in an act of self-creation, places it on his own head.

The moment is captured by the great artist of the revolution, Jacques-Louis David—a man who had been so devoted to Robespierre that he had vowed to "drink hemlock with him" rather than let him die alone. Still alive and sketching furiously, David stands in a recess of Notre Dame. Now it is with Napoleon that he vows to "drink hemlock" if the need should arise.

David quickly produces a bold drawing, a work of genius. In its few strong lines, all that is inessential falls away. It captures Napoleon's inhuman strength of will. One can almost hear the emperor as he holds the crown over his head and proclaims, "God and my sword!"—a soldier's, a knight's credo that interrupts the chanted prayers with a trace of menace.

Afterward, David repeats this sketch a second time while

preparing for his epic painting, *Le Sacre*. In the end, though, David is forced to paint a softer, sentimental moment not to offend Catholic France: Napoleon crowns the kneeling Josephine, her head bowed, her hands clasped in prayer.

But before this compromise is made, David draws another sketch of the self-coronation. In this version, the sword is strapped to a naked torso, for Napoleon is nude. There is no crown, just the naked gesture of reaching upward. There are no royal robes, just the muscular soldier's body that has endured years of hard campaigns. It is this nude sketch which sums up the truth of what Napoleon has achieved. With only his own will on which to rely, out of nothing he has raised himself above popes and kings.

ᴫ ᴫ ᴫ

BUT IF THE world is dazzled by Napoleon, a certain unhappy, ridiculous, sublime—and vulnerable, very vulnerable—eleven-year-old schoolboy in Grenoble is not. Just the opposite: Jean François hates the military spirit sweeping France. He suffers from it. It oppresses him and makes him withdraw into himself, for it permeates every aspect of what he calls his "prison," the *lycée* with its endless army-style parades and its Napoleon-worship.

Everyone in the *lycée* must conform—that is axiomatic in military life. Obedience and inflexible discipline dictate every detail, from how many jacket buttons must be done up and how many left undone, to the 526 books which make up Napoleon's fiat on the curriculum: *these and no others!* It is a restraint terrible to a mind used to ranging where it likes. During Jean François' first weeks he is discovered criminally hiding away a 527th—and a 528th— and a 529th. When the mattresses are restuffed with fresh straw, Persian and Arabic books come tumbling out, Latin poems, a list of Egyptian kings compiled by Manetho in Greek.

Word spreads like wildfire. The incident gives rise to laughter. The new boy is punished, not for hiding away the kind of books usually hidden in the straw—one of the very popular, scurrilous, and illustrated accounts of Marie Antoinette's love life, for example; or a scandalous, lurid novel such as Diderot's *The Nun,* the illicit writing of the day. No, Jean François is made to stand at attention all afternoon for an Arabic grammar and a Persian dictionary and a list of old kings!

For his difference, Jean François will have to endure a ridicule that he never forgets. And though he will later come up against mockery often enough, these early, childish griefs stay with him forever. Years later though occupied with his great work, he will sometimes recall them in letters. He recounts them in detail to his nephew, who leaves them out of his worshipful memoir. For though the schoolboy Jean François has amassed a great deal of precocious learning, still he is less mature than other children of his age and their laughter wounds an innocent nature formed by his solitary upbringing.

But, though his classmates laugh, the authorities take a more serious view. In the masters' view, this hiding of respectable books reflects a rebelliousness, a dangerous independence—not merely a schoolboy's forgivable prurience. By Napoleon's orders, students are instructed under the most rigid constraints. For example, take the question Champollion is asked: *What is the best form of government?*

A universal state like the one Napoleon is creating. Everyone knows this answer. It is repeated often enough by every student—every student, that is, except for the brilliant yet stupid new scholarship boy. Jean François alone refuses to praise Napoleon when called upon in class. Even worse, he gives voice to his own opinions, quoting the classical authors on the tip of his tongue.

Champollion!

A long pause always follows after he is called upon, a silence that lasts forever, though he is self-assured intellectually. It is torture for him to speak in public. It is painful to fully emerge from his intense inner life. His mind, his consciousness is filled with sounds: First and foremost that is how he experiences the languages he studies. A torrent of sounds, soft or harsh, long or short, heavy or light, coming from the throat or the lips, rolled on the palate, or hissed from behind the teeth, combining and recombining like music. "If Arabic is the most beautiful of languages, then Persian is the sweetest, the Italian of the Orient." Each language has a logic and a mystery all its own.

Champollion!

He stands awkwardly in his cracked shoes and the ill-fitting, secondhand uniform his brother bought him, facing the world: his twenty or so classmates.

What is the best form of government?

"The best form of government . . ." he begins, then pauses again. It is unbearable, excruciating. Taking his courage in his hands, he throws himself over the hurdle of his reticence, declaring as a shock goes through the room that he admires republics.

Republics? A few years before it would have been the correct answer, there would have been no other. As Talleyrand cynically remarks: "Treason is a matter of dates." Now with Napoleon having assumed absolute power, such a response could cost Jean François his scholarship.

Not giving this a thought, though, Champollion goes on

to explain why he admires republics—especially the ancient Roman one. He recites Latin epigrams on freedom and lines from Greek poems. His answer is half absurd with its abstruse references—and half sublime. Finally the astonished teacher recollects himself and interrupts with another question: "And what about the glory Napoleon has brought France?"

Again Jean François is ridiculous and sublime. Pale, struggling for breath—on the verge of fainting as is typical of him when he becomes excited—he quotes another classical author: "I love my country, but I love the truth more . . ."

The reply silences the teacher, and earns Jean François two zeros amid shouts of laughter, one for history and one for impudent behavior.

"There are certain incidents which affect the entire course of a student's career in an academic institution," Jacques tells his brother in a reproachful letter. "I have used all my savings and even so, I can barely pay half the costs of keeping you in the *lycée*. Without a scholarship, where would you be? I don't mention the fact that your opinions will be attributed to me. And I don't remind you that by your behavior . . ." But of course he *is* reminding him of what is at stake and he *is* mentioning every fact, every argument he can think of in his effort to make Jean François succeed.

But Jean François is stubborn. He will not, perhaps cannot, give in.

So the teachers quickly come to dislike the poor, arrogant boy with his flashing eyes and his precocious learning, his awkwardness in drill, and his indifference not only to the emperor, but to the great event of the week: the special Sunday dinner, sometimes of sausages, sometimes a fat capon. Even the way Jean François eats his meals makes a bad impression.

His trouble is that he is too much like the emperor he despises. The refusal to lose himself in Napoleon-worship could not be more Napoleonic. For like the emperor, Jean François is passionate, irritable, proud, sensitive, more than a little mad; a visionary.

When he starts to learn Coptic, the language of Egypt in the first centuries after Christ, he gives himself up to his studies so completely that not only does he compile a Coptic dictionary running over two thousand pages, but he himself becomes a Copt: "I think in Coptic," he tells his brother. "I write my notes and keep my accounts and even dream in it."

And when he studies Arabic, he is transformed. Not only are his inflections so perfect that he is indistinguishable from a native Arabic speaker, his voice changes so that even when he speaks French it takes on a throaty and guttural quality. "I barely move my lips when I talk."

Later, this is what sets Jean François apart from other scholars: his emotional, libidinous, voluptuous relationship to ancient language. He is obsessed, driven, stalking his quarry not just with his mind but with all his instinct and passion.

For though his linguistic insights are based on solid scholarship, they are also acts of imagination. If he is a methodical, logical scientist, he is also a magician, a medium through whom ancient Egypt will speak, an artist who lives in the world of his inspirations and who sums up existence thus: "Enthusiasm alone is the true life." Champollion writes the word in Greek letters, conjuring its original meaning: "possessed by the god."

But how to survive in a state *lycée* when you are possessed by a god? If his artistic temperament serves him well in his work, it is an affliction in daily life. He feels every slight or constraint more keenly. The school's routines drive him to despair. He lives for the hours when he can study his "beloved oriental languages" with the learned Abbé Dussert, a special dispensation Jacques has managed to arrange. They are his one joy. His need for these sessions is so strong as to be almost physical. Till the small hours, he pores over his grammars by the dim light of a courtyard lamp, holding the books up on the left side of his bed. The sight in his left eye will be permanently impaired from the strain. By day, he resists anything that takes him away from his languages, cursing the lessons in mathematics and technical drawing, the drills and inspections—"these stupidities."

Hence his endlessly imploring letters to his brother:

"They are killing me with their orders of the day . . .

"I will surely sicken or lose my mind here . . . save me, I beg of you, before that happens . . .

"Set me free," he writes Jacques week after week, month after month, year after year, astonishing letters when one considers that they are written by a young boy lamenting hours "stolen" from the study of languages. At the same time, though, he never forgets the sacrifices Jacques is making to keep him in school. More than that, these sacrifices are a sign of his brother's faith in him, a faith which sustains him. He is ashamed, grateful, and furious all at the same time.

"You see everything through the eyes of a wild horse, as the saying goes: magnified times five," Jacques admonishes. "How will you achieve anything in life if you are ready to die for no reason at all? Besides, I understand that Abbé Dussert is considering permitting you to add another language, either Chaldean or Syriac. *Now* will you be content?"

But of course Jean François is not content: "How can the Abbé make it a question of one or the other? Doesn't he know I must study both? Doesn't he realize"—etc., etc.

He finds a place to be alone. When the others are at meals, Jean François sits under the stairwell and reads Herodotus and Plutarch and Diodorus Siculus, the Greeks and Romans who are Egypt's heirs, and from whom he absorbs everything, whatever is known about Egypt and her gods—the divine vulture Nehkbet, the jackal-god Anubis, and Ra, god of the sun.

Alone in the courtyard of his school, hidden away in an empty classroom, Champollion reads a book in Latin (*The Golden Ass*) by the Greek, Apuleis, praising the Egyptian goddess Isis. He is in the middle of a description of how Isis appeared to author-narrator Apuleis in a vision. Apuleis had been turned into a donkey and had witnessed all the falseness and lusts of the world: the fakery of the eunuch-priests of Isis who take her statue on the road and swindle the people; and then the cruelty of thieves who ride the animal almost to death as they murder and rape. Finally, the donkey manages to eat a garland of roses offered to him by a beautiful nymphomaniac and suddenly he is human again and at the great temple of Isis, worshipping the goddess who has been welcomed into Rome by a people seeking something new: salvation.

"O heart that my mother gave me!" the ex-donkey begins an ancient Egyptian hymn.

"O heart of my different ages!" Apuleis cries out in the work Champollion is reading. And then a military drumroll is heard throughout the school, followed by an even harsher, more dream-destroying bugle call: *ra-ta-ta!* Another parade, another drill and inspection: Is the angle of Champollion's hat correct? His back straight? Arms at the sides?

Darkness. Despair. The end of the world.

To put it in the words of his beloved Apuleis—that man-turned-donkey-turned-man-again by grace of Egypt's gods—the problem is *Et hic adhus infantilis uterus gestat nobis infantem aliem*. . . . This is a prophecy addressed to Psyche, to Mind, a young girl who has coupled with Eros or Love: *Though you are still only a child, you will soon have a child of your own* . . .

Within Jean François, mind has also joined with passion. And though he too is young, he is heavy with intellectual child.

Chapter Five

Lions of the Desert

*Grenoble. The residence of the prefect
(that is, governor) of the Department of Isère.*

ON AN AFTERNOON toward the beginning of
spring in 1803, an unusual scene takes place at the prefect's
official residence. A schoolboy—Jean François—makes his
appearance among the throng of petitioners and men of
affairs in the prefect's waiting room. He is received right
away. While government business is forgotten, the prefect
and Jean François sit talking—or, rather, Jean François listens as the prefect talks, trying to put the tense, silent boy at
ease.

The prefect is new to his job. He does not look the part:
His skin is dark and leathery from long treks in the Egyp-

tian deserts, forced marches which many did not survive. He is still gaunt from the dysentery endemic among the troops. For he is none other than Jean Baptiste Fourier, physicist and secretary of the savants in Egypt, a scientist Napoleon put in a political post because he needs someone he can trust.

Though Fourier is no politician, he has been dealing ably with the throng of visitors crowding his waiting room, the clever lawyers and greedy contractors and ambitious bureaucrats who come to see him about every kind of business—every kind that is, except the one closest to the prefect's heart: the many-volumed *Description of Egypt,* which it is now his privilege to help create.

It is a Herculean task. The savants have collected a vast wealth of knowledge, statistics, maps, specimens, and a thick portfolio of drawings, the bulk by the artist Dominique Denon. Nothing escapes Denon's eye: the geometrical splendor of a temple, the claws of a bat clinging to a palm, and countless inscriptions. They appear as long strings of hieroglyphs seen not only on monuments but in Cairo's back alleys, by the quays of Alexandria, in the fields of peasants, where huge, ancient stones have been quarried from the ruins.

Inscribed with images of kings and gods, these stones laden with knowledge now prop up a bathhouse or a privy. Covered with unreadable texts, epic poems, spells, and prayers, they are now used to grind the newly harvested grain.

The Shabaka stone records the wisdom of the famed school of Heliopolis ('Ηλιου πολεως "City of the Sun," as the Greeks called it, 𓉔 𓊖 "Iunu" for the Egyptians and אוֹן "On" in the Bible: a place ancient even in the days when Joseph spoke with Pharaoh). Here is four-thousand-year-old philosophical speculation, lectures attended by Plato and Pythagoras, the cosmogony of the priests of Ra. Now dragged round and round by donkeys, its contents forgotten, the stone's surface is pitted with holes and scratches, its metaphysics covered with coarse Nubian millet and bits of straw.

To this chaos of half-understood, half-rescued knowledge, Fourier must bring order. He comes to this task after days spent on government business, listening to officials seeking promotions, engineers planning roads through the mountains and wrangling churchmen—bishops, priests, worldly, difficult men fighting for what is due the church, the power that was theirs before the revolution. (Napoleon's "I treat the pope as if he had two hundred thousand men!" is all that Fourier has to go by.) Not to mention the lawyers who also have a claim on Fourier's time. He must review cases so vexed it is a wonder that he can work at all on the *Description of Egypt,* that the violent stories and faces of those condemned to die do not come between him and the page.

All of this—the criminals at the Place d'Armes, *and* military reviews, *and* tours of inspection—rests on Fourier's shivering shoulders (for he is subject to bouts of malarial fever, a souvenir he has brought back with him from Egypt, from the swampy Fayum, along with his spoils, the beautiful and moving antiquities he has acquired). Worn out by his duties and his maladies, how is it that this visitor of Fourier's—a mere child! a schoolboy!—will lift his spirits so?

They meet by chance when the prefect comes to visit the *lycée*. A fateful chance, the ancient Egyptians would have dialectically called it because, despite the difference in their age and situations, it is impossible that two such kindred spirits should live in the same city and not know each other.

Fate throws them together in Grenoble and keeps them together forever. When they die, they will lie near each other under Egyptian-style monuments in the Père Lachaise cemetery. And even in the twentieth century, valleys named after them when the moon is explored will not be far apart.

What then was the teacher at the *lycée* thinking of that day? Did he imagine that by putting Jean François in the back row to hide his shabby uniform he could prevent the "Egyptian" prefect from noticing the "Egyptian" boy?

It is not just that Jean François knows *something* about Egypt. All the students have followed Napoleon's campaigns, some have even heard firsthand accounts from relatives in the army of the battle of the pyramids, the Cairo uprising, and the siege at Acre. But Egypt has been Jean François' imaginative home. When questioned by Fourier, not only does he answer, but he eagerly asks the prefect his own questions. He talks with intimate knowledge, ranging over place and time with such ease that finally Fourier can only exclaim, "Who has been in Egypt, this boy or me?"

Fourier invites Jean François—not the indignant teacher and not the distinguished head of the *lycée*—to visit him at the prefecture. Talking to the boy as an equal, as Champollion will later remember, he inquires in the polite language of the day whether Jean François will *do him the honor* of paying him a visit.

Then the prefect is gone and Jean François is alone in the *lycée* again—no longer a savant but a boy who cannot spell or do the simplest math problems and who has had the impudence to hold forth before such an important visitor. Of course this "unseemly self-display" will be forgiven later on when the learned societies and the *lycée* will fight to claim Jean François as their own, this student in a shabby uniform who did not even have the manners to thank the prefect for his invitation—disgraceful!—who did not have the sense to take Fourier's extended hand but stood unsmiling, staring and speechless, self-conscious and overwhelmed.

Overwhelmed or not, Jean François accepts Fourier's invitation and so it comes to pass that the two sit closeted together in the prefect's office. The meeting will be a turning point in Jean François' young life.

Fourier inquires about Jean François' studies, about his home and family in Figeac—his questions go unanswered. At first Jean François is unable to say a word. So the prefect then talks about Egypt. He describes scenes that have not changed since the time of Herodotus and before: a water boy sitting astride his ox, his *gallibaya* tucked up, his bare thin legs straddling the massive flanks of the patient animal. The boy's song, *Ya Amuni! Ya Amuni!* has been passed down for generations, the words of the ancient language having become more and more incomprehensible and distorted until only these two syllables are left—Amun, "the Hidden God." These syllables no longer conveying this or any other meaning, have become nothing more than plaintive and melancholy sound, something for a boy to sing as he and his ox work the *shaduf*.

The boy sings, the ox lows, and the buckets of the *shaduf* rise and dip, filling an irrigation ditch where, together with his horse, a man washes off the day's toil . . .

It is a scene from the present, from the past, from a mural in an eighteenth dynasty tomb. The water buckets of the *shaduf* were rising and falling even then. Or rather: they rise and fall even now. In Egypt, the past is real and the present is not. The past overshadows the present, making it seem like a dream.

Fourier tells the boy about the tomb of Sennefer, mayor of Wast. Its walls are covered with fields and vineyards painted in brilliant colors, with harvesters and flocks of wild birds, resurrection spells and naked dancing girls: sinuous bodies so beautiful that they alone could resurrect the mayor . . . if his mummy had not been used for fuel, that is! Tossed onto the fire one cold desert night to warm his descendants.

In the fields, herds of goats trample newly sown grain into the soil, just as they did in the days of pharaoh. And in the Egyptian churches metal rattles still echo during mass: *sistra-so* the Greeks called them; הֲתֹף *hatof* to the Hebrews. It is the instrument Miriam played at the Red Sea when she led the women in song; *sesheshet* to the ancient Egyptians, a word whose sound was meant to capture a rattle's tinkling, which in turn was meant to capture the sound of papyrus stalks rustling in the wind. *Sistra, tofim, sesheshet*—these instruments that joyous, bare-breasted girls once used to appease the erotic rage of the cow goddess Hathor now in the hands of bearded monks solemnly worshipping a child suckling at the Virgin's breast, just as the hawk-headed Horus suckled at the breast of Isis.

Everywhere: past and present, life and death mingle with bittersweet pathos. The baby glove of a pharaoh is all that remains in an empty tomb. Nearby, flowers have been strewn by ancient mourners: acacia blossoms and lotus petals, persea leaves and poppy petals, garlands which, when touched by the breath of the living, crumble into dust.

In the midst of this all-pervasive past, the boisterous, immodest, irreverent French arrive. Their heads are filled with the ideas of Voltaire and Rousseau. The *Marseillaise* on their drunken lips, they revel in the streets of Cairo or ride out to the countryside.

Conquerors—for the hour, at least—they race camels in the desert and wrestle alligators on the banks of the Nile. Naked, covered with mud, they shout with excitement as they gouge the beasts' eyes. Their sport watched at a distance by barefoot women veiled in black, whose thick gold ankle bracelets flash in the sun.

It is a different world the prefect describes to Jean François; a land, Napoleon will say of Egypt later, where he was able to shake off the constraints of European civilization, a place to feel joyous and free. But that is how the Emperor remembers it later, after he has lost his empire, in exile on a bleak pacific island. Then, suffering from piles and skin rashes, from scurvy and seizures and swelling of the legs, it is natural for one or another of the otherworldly Egyptian scenes the artist Denon has sketched to conjure happier memories.

Then even the ex-Emperor's sugar bowl evokes the glorious Egyptian campaign. Sèvres porcelain, it is also designed by Denon, with a vivid depiction on its sides: stark cliffs surrounding the Nile at Elephantine. "Greatness has its beauties," as Napoleon himself will admit, "but only in memory and only in retrospect."

The truth is that suffering dogs the steps of the French in Egypt. A hush falls over the men as they sight shore, an empty stretch of desert some eight miles east of Alexandria. The fear and foreboding of the soldiers is more in keeping with the fate awaiting them than their general's feelings of "freedom and joy."

Realistically, Fourier describes the arduous campaign to Jean François. For though the prefect admires Napoleon, he has witnessed the events with the cold eye of a scientist. His point of view is closer to that of the grumbling men than to Napoleon's.

From the first, nature is hostile. Rocky shoals make it impossible to bring the large ships close to shore. Napoleon orders them to be anchored where they are. The skies have been darkening all afternoon, and now strong winds whip up the waves as a skiff rows out to greet them. It is the French consul who has been anxiously awaiting their arrival, his lookouts posted all along the coast. Buffeted by the winds and clinging to the lines thrown down to him, the consul—a comical figure in formal clothes and drenched to the skin—is drawn aboard the *Orient*.

He closets himself with Napoleon to tell him the news: The English have already arrived in Egypt, a vastly superior naval force under Nelson. And though they have come and gone in hot pursuit, they will surely soon realize their mistake and return.

Indeed, even as the consul speaks, an officer interrupts with the news that a warship has been seen on the horizon—perhaps the first of many.

"Fortune, why have you abandoned me?" Napoleon cries with anguish, rushing on deck. "Five days is all I ask!"

It is not the English: only *Justice,* a French ship that had lagged behind and is now rejoining the fleet.

Still there is no time to lose, Napoleon realizes. The English might return any moment. To meet them at sea would mean disaster. He must get his men on land right away, despite the heavy swell, the high winds, and the darkness.

As the sun sets over the stormy sea, he is everywhere at once, giving a hundred orders, urging his men on, raging one moment, cold and precise the next. In a crisis, he is completely the military man. He forgets the savants: They are not the priority. Neighing horses are now suddenly more important than the philosophers.

"I began by landing six horses," Anne-Jean-Marie

Savary, the officer in charge of the operation, will remember, "placing the horsemen in a boat, and letting the horses down into the sea, each dragoon holding his horse by a halter.

"The first horse thus removed from the ship swam in place until the last had been let down into the sea; after which the boat made for shore, towing the six horses that were swimming, and placing them on land as near as possible to the water's edge so the other horses could see them . . . and follow in the same manner.

"Horses of each vessel were hoisted out on both sides at once and let down into the sea while a boat was in readiness to lead them gently to overtake the others . . . a long file of horses swimming toward shore."

Horses fare better than the men. ". . . The violent wind churned up the sea," General Louis-Alexandre Berthier remembers, "making it impossible to navigate our boats, creating a gale that heaved one boat on top of another, smashing some, overturning others and hurling men into the foaming surf far from shore . . ."

It is a scene from a nightmare: the commands of officers shouted over howling winds, surfboats and sloops packed with soldiers tossing on the high waves, foundering on the reefs; the struggle in the darkness amid the cries of the drowning; the black beach where horses rear with terror. Hundreds die.

The scene may resemble a nightmare but it is *Napoleon's* nightmare they are living. At three in the morning, Napoleon appears on the beach to review those troops who have managed to reach land.

He brushes aside obstacles that would give another commander pause. Have there been heavy casualties? In war, death is a matter of course. As Antoine Lasalle, his favorite cavalry leader, puts it: "A hussar not dead at thirty is a bungler."

Is it impossible to hoist down the heavy artillery? Have most provisions—the dry biscuit and water—been left on the ships? Well, they can worry about that later on.

The main thing is to get started. War brings into play all Napoleon's enormous energy, all his will and imagination. He is in high spirits as he sets off for Alexandria, shouting bawdy jokes over the still raging wind. He sings snatches of Italian songs in the dark desert, holding forth on women, art, wine, law, and religion, issuing orders as they occur to him ("There is to be no looting, no pillaging . . . Respect the mosques as you would a church . . . Approach all wells with care: They may be poisoned . . .")

The band, safely ashore, strikes up the *Marseillaise* to lend fresh courage to the exhausted and storm-tossed men. They are surrounded by shadows, by Bedouin waiting to capture stragglers whom they rape and mutilate before putting to death.

Thus with the groans of the dying, with the revolutionary anthem in the background, with bawdy jokes, bravery and fear, the conquest of Egypt begins.

⌐⌐ ⌐⌐ ⌐⌐

JEAN FRANÇOIS COMES to life, his imagination most deeply stirred when Fourier finally shows him his "treasures"—his *ostraca* first of all: potsherds, shattered bowls, water jugs, and wine jars broken millennia ago by a careless slave or naughty child, its pieces kept for scrap paper. Bits of clay and flakes of limestone covered with ancient writing: Greek and Aramaic and, oldest of all, hieroglyphs. The fragments speak to Jean François in a way that the prefect's tales of glory and hardship do not.

The French schoolboy holds the work of another schoolboy in his hands. The hieroglyphs are awkwardly drawn on the clay and an outline in red has been traced around them—a teacher's corrections of a clumsy attempt.

The writing on the other antiquities, however, is anything but clumsy. For not only the *ostraca* but the statues and papyrus scrolls and jewelry are covered with images meant for the eye as well as the mind. The hieroglyphs are painted in brilliant colors or engraved with exquisite care. The quivering antennae of a bee, the body of a woman squatting in childbirth, a thousand sensuous details occur and reoccur according to the logic of a forgotten language that, once deciphered, will be seen to have recorded everything.

There are magical formulas and mathematical problems and medical advice: lists of remedies and detailed, accurate descriptions of all parts of the anatomy. "They laid open men while alive—criminals received out of prison from the king—and while they still breathed they study them." The brain, *nt nt,* meninges:　is drawn out through the nose during embalming in a delicate operation requiring a small perforation—less than two centimeters—through the ethmoid bone. The embalmer's knowledge is shared with the doctors, as can be seen in mummies with evidence of trepanning performed on them during their lifetime, operations—*dua,* knife treatments:　to relieve *besy,* swelling:　.
Judging from the healed bone tissue in the mummified skulls these procedures must have been successful.

This is what is written on the *ostraca* and papyrus rolls and is waiting to be deciphered. A whole world now silent is encoded in the magical-seeming hieroglyphs: lyrical poems and prayers as well as prosaic records, property demarcations, and criminal cases, transcripts moldering in temple archives as they do in courthouses today.

But perhaps the most absorbing document of all, the one which makes one truly aware of what is at stake in the decipherment—our sense of our human past, of ourselves, of our unalterable human condition—is the story of a royal prince and high priest of Memphis in 1230 BC, Khaem-waset.

When the boy Champollion, tentatively touching the papyrus fragments with his clumsy, trembling fingers, grows into the linguist he will be, Prince Khaemwaset will emerge from his long sleep with a long, dark scream. Call it magic, call it existential despair, this shriek from 1230 BC might have been painted in the twentieth century by the Norwegian artist Munch.

One of the 111 sons of Ramesses II, Khaemwaset was restlessly, reflectively drawn to the past. A brooding, royal scholar versed in the wisdom of his day, he haunted his ancestors' ruined palaces and tombs. In a still extant inscription high on a pyramid's side, he declares that it was he, Khaemwaset, who restored the crumbling pyramid of Unas, a pharaoh who reigned in 2375 BC, a thousand years before.

And what does Khaemwaset discover in his researches? A chant carved on the walls of Unas' forgotten tomb that celebrates a brutality long erased from Egyptian civiliza-tion: cannibalism.

Unas is the bull of heaven who rages in his heart!
Who lives on the being of every god,
Who eats their entrails.
Unas is he who eats men, feeds on gods . . .

—so goes the savage chant from the tomb of the fifth dynasty pharaoh Prince Khaemwaset restores.

Thus Khaemwaset, having delved into the past, becomes a figure of awe in the papyri which tell his story. He is said to have a knowledge that is more than human, to be a magician, a kind of demigod. While epic poems celebrate the conquests of his father, Ramesses II, his son Khaemwaset is known neither for subduing the Hittite legions nor slaying the fierce Meshwesh of the desert. No, his life finds its ideal in the search for a book.

It is an ancient volume compiled by the ibis-headed god of writing himself: a book, we are told, which had once belonged to a kindred spirit of Khaemwaset's, to a Prince Neferkaptah, to whom it had brought grief many generations earlier. Right away this plot thickens: The ancient story of Prince Khaemwaset's search for knowledge throws us back into an even more remote time in a Kafkaesque search for a truth "at the bottom of a bottomless well."

Where is Khaemwaset to find this book? Who was this Neferkaptah, also a prince and the book's long-dead owner? In a fragment from one papyrus, a voice suddenly speaks to us from this remote past, the sister of Neferkaptah and the daughter of the pharaoh. She is frightened at the prospect of her brother being given another woman to wed and of another man being given to her as husband. It is incest— told so innocently that one is touched by the simplicity of this faraway voice describing the brother whom she loved:

> In the time of my father . . . the Pharaoh grew old and had no children but my elder brother, Neferkaptah and I . . . Pharaoh wanted children from his children and made a feast, inviting the sons and daughters of the generals in order that Pharaoh might choose a husband for me and a wife for his son Nefer-kaptah . . .

> A steward, an aged man told this to us and we became sad and very afraid, for we loved one another exceedingly . . . and I went to the steward and said: "Ask Pharaoh not to part us, for we love each other very much . . ." And Pharaoh became angry . . .

In another fragment, she speaks of herself as her brother's wife—Pharaoh must have relented. She is now also the mother of a child, *Beloved Heart:*

> My brother-husband Neferkaptah had no occupation but to study in the schools of the House of Life [among the scribes]

and to walk in the cemetery of Memphis, reading the writing on the tombs and writing on other monuments and his zeal was great. But one day while he was walking behind a procession in honor of the god Ptah, he was reading the writing on the shrines and an old priest saw him and laughed.

"Why are you reading writings which have no importance? Come, I will show you what Thoth wrote with his own hand."

And he brought him to a tomb where the book shed light, light as strong as the sun . . .

This is the magical book which the historical Khaemwaset seeks. If myth mingles with fact in its description, this is to emphasize the danger. For Solomon's warning, "He who increases wisdom, increases sorrow" was a proverb in Egypt a thousand years before Solomon. And Egyptians did not need a Hebrew God to teach them that to taste of the fruit of the tree of knowledge was to taste of death.

Finally, in a scroll reused many times—perhaps one in which business accounts had been recorded and then washed away, so that here and there the old writing could still be seen, one layer on top of another with the new hieroglyphs barely readable in places—thus Khaemwaset, for all his immersion in the priestly archives, all his researches and restorations, gives himself up to lust.

It happened one day that Setne [the priestly title by which Khaemwaset refers to himself] was strolling in the forecourt of the temple of Ptah. Then he saw a woman who was very beautiful, there being no other woman like her in appearance. The moment Setne saw her, he did not know where he was. He called his man servant, saying: "Run to the place where this woman is, and find out who she is."

The man servant ran to the place where the woman was. He called to the maid servant following her and asked: "What woman is this?"

She told him: "It is Tabeh, the daughter of the prophet of Bastet, mistress of Ankhtawi. She has come here to worship Ptah, the great god."

When the man servant returned and related her words, Setne ordered: "Go, say, 'It is Setne Khaemwaset, the son of Pharaoh Usermare, who has sent me to say: "I will give you gold—spend an hour with me. Or do you have a complaint of wrongdoing? I will have it settled for you." ' "

The servant returned to the place where Tabeh was. He called her maid and told her. She cried out as if what he said was an insult. Tabeh said to the man servant: "Stop talking to this foolish girl. Come and speak with me."

The servant told her Setne's words and she answered: "Go, tell Setne, I am of priestly rank. I am not a low person. If you desire to do what you wish with me, you must come to Bubastis, to my house. There you shall do what you wish with me, without anyone on earth finding me."

When Setne heard her words, he had a boat brought and hastened to Bubastis. When he came to the west of the city he found a lofty house with a wall around it, a garden on its north and a seat at its door. Setne went inside the wall and they announced him to Tabeh.

She came down, took Setne's hand and said to him: "By the welfare of the house of the prophet of Bastet, mistress of Ankhtawi, which you have reached, it will please me greatly if you come up."

Setne walked up the stairs of the house with Tabeh. He found the upper story adorned with lapis lazuli and turquoise. A gold cup was filled with wine and put into Setne's hand. Setne said: "Let me do what I have come to do."

She answered: "I am of priestly rank. I am not a low person. If you desire to do what you wish with me, you must write for me a deed for everything you own."

He said: "Send for the scribe."

He was brought at once. He made a deed of maintenance and of compensation in money for everything, all goods belonging to him.

Setne said: "Tabeh, let me do what I have come here for!"

She said to him: "If you desire to do what you wish with me, you must make your children sign the deed. Do not leave them to contend with my children over your property."

He had his children brought and made them sign the deed.

Tabeh rose and put on a garment of royal linen. Setne saw all her limbs through it and his desire became even greater than it had been before. He said: "Let me do what I have come to do."

Tabeh answered: "If you desire to do what you wish with me, you must have your children killed. Do not leave them to contend with my children over your property."

Setne said: "Let the abomination be done."

She had his children killed before him. She had them thrown down from the window to the dogs. They ate their flesh, and he heard them as he drank with Tabeh.

Setne said: "Let us do what we have come here for! All the things that you have said, I have done."

She said: "Come now."

He lay down on a couch of ivory and ebony, he stretched out
his arms, and Tabeh lay down beside him. As he touched her,
she opened her mouth wide in a loud cry. Setne awakened in
a state of great heat, no clothes on him, his phallus hard.

This is the dream of desire and revulsion Khaemwaset
sought in the old, old book—the book written by the god
of writing and hidden in the ancient tomb of Neferkaptah:
Khaemwaset steals it at his peril.

Opposed to his father Ramesses' massive images of
power and order, to the huge temples at Abu Simbel and
Karnak, to the poem of Pentaur, which praises Ramesses'
military might, Khaemwaset's dream is like the howling of
the hyenas in the desert at night, or the desert sands which
Khaemwaset contemplates as he prowls the ancient ruins
of his ancestor's tombs. It is like the god of the desert himself, Seth, engaged in deadly combat with his nephew
Horus.

The prince's dream represents chaos opposed to the
great social order with its pyramids, both human and stone,
from the top of which the dead pharaoh ascends to the
heavens. It represents the complex human imagination,
sensing something ancient and dangerous and *sacred* and
forbidden at the beginning of time. Murderous or canni-
balistic urges transformed, through ritual, into a tame echo
of itself.

And thus Khaemwaset with his searching for the past, though he himself is near the beginnings of (dynastic, recorded, historical) time, is like a gravedigger using natal forceps to bury us, at birth, in modern angst and nihilistic woe.

ꟷ ꟷ ꟷ

IN FOURIER'S STUDY, Jean François wanders among the ancient objects covered with writing. He sees a fragment from a young man's coffin, late, from the Roman period. His portrait has been painted, in encaustic: the pigments burned into the wood, on a gilded mask meant to cover his mummy. The youth's black hair is a thick tangle of rough curls falling over his forehead, the barbarian style fashionable in the first century AD. His eyes are large and staring. Sparse beginnings of a beard cover his downy cheeks.

Next to him is another Roman-period coffin, a complete one of lime wood with a young girl portrayed on the mask.

Her cheekbones are high, her skin a warm pinkish apricot. Her white mantle and her jewelry—three gold snake bracelets—have been carelessly painted. From the left, light falls on her young face with its melancholy expression. Thick, red lips, a half frown. Large dark eyes look sadly to a point beyond the viewer. A garland of rosebuds encircle dark hair pulled back with a severity more in keeping with an older face.

Around the sides of the coffin and on the sides of the headrest under the girl's neck, spells have been painted in brilliant colors, hieroglyphs invoking the gods of Egypt. Soon, in two centuries, they too will undergo the oblivion of death, their altars covered with sand or usurped by monks living in the desert.

Running his hand over the writing, Jean François asks the prefect if anyone knows what it means. Fourier shakes his head. A stone has been found in the course of reinforcing an old fort at el-Rashid (Rosetta)—an ancient decree written in both hieroglyphs and Greek. But the meaning of the hieroglyphs is still as obscure as the spells painted on the young girl's coffin.

"Then I will be the one!" Jean François declares with a fervor Fourier will never forget. "I will decipher the hieroglyphs . . ."

PART

II

Chapter Six

To the Strongest!

1799.

FROM A MILITARY point of view, the first stages of the French campaign in Egypt—the taking of Alexandria and the other ports along the coast, Damietta and Rosetta—are not all that significant. The main battle, the so-called Battle of the Pyramids, will take place before Cairo. It is this encounter that will be decisive (or as decisive as anything may be said to be in Egypt!).

From another point of view, perhaps the point of view of eternity, the most important event occurs during the dog days of August in 1799, at Rosetta, a sleepy port where a branch of the Nile empties into the Mediterranean.

The town surrenders to the French without a battle.

They have heard of the fall of Alexandria (some thirty miles to the west).

The French commander, General Menou, though suffering from wounds sustained at Alexandria, is active in surveying the military possibilities, choosing suitable bivouacs and requisitioning provisions and deciding, in the course of an inspection, to turn the ruined fort at the edge of town into a French stronghold. He gives orders for soldiers to begin work on its walls right away.

Then he changes his mind and puts it off, so for a while longer the abandoned fort remains undisturbed in the blazing sun by the sea, its mud-brick walls indistinguishable from any others.

And when the French soldiers finally do arrive with their pickaxes and shovels, they report that nomads have taken shelter here. Naked children and goats scamper in the rubble. Robust desert women sing wordless songs, old men snooze in the shade while young ones walk by the sea, planning their endless blood feuds.

Some parts of the wall are strong, but others must be cleared away. The soldiers' axes rise and fall, hour after hour, day after day. The monotonous work continues as the children shout and run among them, a much-appreciated distraction for the lonely, toiling men. Just beneath the crumbling brick, an axe blow away is *the* stone. Made up of hard quartz-bearing rock and feldspar and mica, it will shimmer in the sun. Not yet black but dark gray with a delicate vein of pink, the Rosetta stone lies waiting to be discovered . . .

口 口 口

INSCRIBED WITH A long-forgotten decree from a long-forgotten world, the stone found at Rosetta is as distant from Egypt's glorious past as it is from the Frenchmen digging in the sun. By the time of the decree (196 BC), the Egypt of the Old Kingdom pyramids has ended. The powerful Middle and New Kingdoms are over. Gone forever are the pharaohs whose every nod or frown made the kings of the east tremble and at whose command great temples rose, even in times of famine.

Now they lie together in a jumble like so many numbered corpses in a morgue—kings, queens, princes, great officials, and courtiers. In the dead of night, they are secretly carried from their splendid tombs by pious, grieving priests trying to save their desecrated bodies.

Their mummies are rewrapped in coarse strips of cloth. Robbers have destroyed their royal shrouds, cutting to the very bone in their search for gold and silver. Placed in simple wooden coffins—or coffinless, stacked against the wall of a cave hidden deep in the desert cliffs—they will lie there for two thousand years until, astonished and unbelieving, archaeologists stumble upon them in the late nineteenth century: princes in a pauper's grave. It is a royal potter's field, an ironic end for those who lavished all their wealth, all their subjects' strength on their burials, but it is the most the priests can do.

For they no longer have the power to guard the splendidly carved and painted tombs that once housed these dead yet living gods. These priests risk their lives simply by performing this last humble act for the kings they still worship, pharaohs whose immortal *Ka*—soul, spirit, double— they still nourish with offerings of calves' liver and honeyed bread and aged palm wine.

By 196 BC, Egypt has become a shadow of itself, a land ruled by foreigners for so long that the Egyptian on the stone must be carved both in the half-forgotten hieroglyphs and demotic, a new, scrawled form of the language. There are carvings in Greek as well, for by this time, Egyptian by itself no longer suffices. The hapless Egyptian scribe who struggles to translate the Greek of the decree into hieroglyphs sometimes leaves out words, clumsily paraphrasing or completely changing turns of phrases difficult to write in Egyptian, phrases more natural in the foreign language of his Greek master—Ptolemy V, called Ptolemy *Epiphanes,* that is, *The Appearance of the God* in Greek— "who is exceedingly glorious, who has established Egypt firmly, who is beloved of men and gods, who—" etc.

And who, as the decree does not mention, in reality is a sad boy-king whose father, Ptolemy IV, spurred on by his whores and catamites, killed his mother. Her melancholy nature bored him! No older than thirteen, Ptolemy V is suddenly elevated to the throne by the death of his father. Whereupon eunuch-guardians corrupt the young Ptolemy, enslaving him to pleasure so that they may rule in his stead.

There is pathos in the story behind the decree, a pathos which, moreover, is useful in the decipherment of the stone on which it is written: for in decipherment, *all* decipherment—ancient decrees, modern military codes, even secret lovers' notes—context plays as great a part as word-for-word evidence. The linguist must have some feeling for the world of the document, some knowledge of the circumstances surrounding the message he is trying to decipher.

When Young, Champollion's British rival, works on the stone, he is primarily concerned with analyzing the number of times such and such a sign repeats itself. Champollion draws upon his imagination, his intuitive faculties as well as his analytic ones.

Unlike Young, a man of varied interests, Champollion has immersed himself in Egypt and he knows and knows and knows. A pillar inscribed in Greek near the Red Sea, a papyrus from a temple by the Nile, pieced together, describe this *Epiphanes,* this *Appearance of the God* in a hundred different moments, any one of which may—or may not!—help unlock an obscure sentence or a difficult phrase: the trembling Greek boy crowned Ptolemy in ancient incomprehensible Egyptian ceremonies; the adolescent King Ptolemy who hunts in the delta swamps for weeks at a time, neglecting affairs of state as he pursues the rhino and wild bird, obsessed with the chase—traveling far to the south to capture elephants and kill panthers and the gazelles that run in large herds in the wilderness; the arrogant young ruler Ptolemy who falls asleep as foreign ambassadors make their speeches and who, awakened by his former tutor, the aged Aristomenes, has the old man put to death.

There are many sources which bring to life not only Ptolemy V but the entire Greek Egypt of this epoch. There are many pictures of that violent, incestuous, intellectual, pleasure-loving dynasty, the Ptolemies, who by the time of the decree have degenerated. They are nothing like the hardy, practical Ptolemy I, the dynasty's founder.

For by 196 BC, it is late not only in Egyptian history but late even in the history of her Greek conquerors who—

despite being born in Egypt for century after century—
continue to speak only Greek and to be known by Greek,
not Egyptian names—Ptolemy *Epiphanes, Eucharistos*
(praised), Ptolemy *Euergetes* (performer of good deeds),
Ptolemy *Philadelphus* (brother/sister loving)—and even by
Greek nicknames—*Auletes* (flute player), *Physcon* (fatty),
Lathyrus (chickpea), etc. Greek titles have replaced the titles of the previous dynasty—which was also foreign—
Persian—and which also used foreign languages on its inscriptions (Darius' Nile–Red Sea canal, for example, is
commemorated in quadralinguals: Persian, Elamite, Baby-
lonian, the languages of the Persian empire, *and* Egyptian).

For the Greeks are not the first to conquer Egypt: by 196
BC, defeat has followed defeat. The Persians had arrived first
(in 525 BC), humbling and oppressing the people, defiling
the temples and mocking the gods whose gold and silver
images they steal. They kill the sacred animals and desecrate
the tombs: Unrolling the mummies of those pharaohs they
can find, Herodotus reports, they crush their bones, burning what will burn and tossing the rest onto dung heaps.
The all-important irrigation ditches are allowed to silt up,
priests are degraded and starving people raise their hands at
broken altars.

For a brief interval, the Egyptians rise up and drive out
the foreigners (380 BC), establishing the thirtieth dynasty,
which struggles to revive the ancient glory.

That is soon over. By 343 BC the Persians have returned in force. The last pharaoh of Egyptian blood, Nectanebo II, flees to the far reaches of the south where he lives in seclusion, devoting the rest of his life to magic and esoteric meditations. He can be seen on temple friezes, naked and bald, holding bowls of incense as he kneels before "the coffins of the unborn gods" and offering up unheard prayers for Egypt.

Or perhaps they are heard after all. Perhaps Egypt's salvation paradoxically lies in its destruction. Like an overripe fruit, it must fall from the tree and burst open, its seed scattering to the winds, its wisdom taking new forms. To be sure, this is the Egypt that Alexander the Great conquers with his Greeks in 332 BC: a fallen, pillaged land.

He is greeted as a liberator. Memphis opens its gates to him with joy, priests anoint him with the sacred oils and adorn him with the god Amun's ram-horns (on coins, they can be seen beneath his thick Greek curls). He is declared pharaoh. But for the short time Alexander remains in Egypt, he is a *Greek* pharaoh—or rather, a Macedonian bearing Greek ideals: for he is from that rugged land just to the north of Greece. He is a Macedonian who has been formed by his tutor Aristotle and the epics of Homer.

Unlike the Persians before him, Alexander scrupulously honors Egypt's gods. Yet at the same time he forcibly turns her center of being from the inward-looking life of the

Nile valley to the shores of the Mediterranean where he founds Alexandria, a city that will not only become Egypt's new capital but a cosmo-polis, a city of the world.

It is a city—no, more an *idea* than a city—that will astonish the ancient world. Here, while its power-mad kings and queens get caught up in endless, remorseless struggles, while royal blood flows in streams from the palace by the sea, Euclid will formulate the principles of geometry. The polymath Erastothenes (in 276 BC), *assuming that the world is round,* and basing his calculations on nothing more than the angles of shadows cast by the sun, will determine the circumference of the earth accurate to within fifty miles.

The kings themselves—Ptolemy VIII, for example—will turn to intellectual speculation. At the end of a sixty-eight-year reign, Ptolemy VIII holds forth on natural history, of which he is a keen observer if the surviving fragments of his many-volumed work are any indication. He writes a treatise on political wisdom as well, of which he must have possessed an uncommon measure. For he was able to patch up his quarrel with his wife Cleopatra II (it had plunged the country into civil war). And though he had previously taken his revenge on her by murdering their son Memphites, his reign ends in peace and contentment, his two wives, Cleopatra II, the mother, and Cleopatra III, her daughter (from another brother), by his side.

Here at Alexandria, amid crime and cerebration, fires seem to scorch the skies: the seventy-foot-high Pharos—huge mirrors magnifying its light—will guide ships into the harbor for more than a thousand years, one of the seven wonders of the ancient world.

The greatest library that the world has ever known draws scholars and poets from the ends of the earth. Its Museum, home of the muses, attracts scientists and historians (and clever priests who study the principles of hydrostatics and the properties of magnets to create "miracles" in their temples: singing statues and gods who fly through the air).

Here, later, the Christian heretic Arius and the orthodox Athansius will struggle to define Christ's nature, *homoiousian,* like God's; or *homoousian,* the same as God's; debating over the diphthong with a ferocious hatred and a violence, and a brilliance unsurpassed in Church history. They take turns fleeing to the desert to save their lives until Arius dies on the streets of the city during a prolonged epileptic fit.

All of this is yet to be: When Alexander first sees "the city" it is a spit of land jutting out into the sea and forming a double harbor. Envisioning its possibilities, the newly victorious conqueror comes ashore and strides east and west and north and south, marking boundaries, indicating where walls are to rise with such swift decision, such impetuosity, that his men can find nothing with which to mark the new city lines but a sack of barley they scatter in his Promethean footsteps.

Birds swoop down and eat up the barley. This "evil omen" would have led Alexander to abandon his plan if a soothsayer had not declared it a sign that the city would feed the world. Then the young "pharaoh" is gone: "For a longing had seized Alexander," the ancient historian Arrian tells us, "to consult the god Amun [at the remote oasis of Siwa], for his oracle was known to be infallible.

"As far as Paraetonium [modern Mersah Matruh] he went along the coast," Arrian continues, "a distance of sixteen hundred stades. There he turned into the interior, where the oracle was. The route is desolate; most of it is sand and waterless. Whenever a south wind blows in that country, it makes a great heap of sand on the route and obscures its marks, making it impossible to get one's bearings . . ."

Here at the temple of Amun-Ra, the Egyptian priest and his new master enter the holy of holies where Alexander has come with three questions:

Has the murder of his father been avenged?

Will he conquer the world?

And is he himself a god?

Yes, yes, yes, the oracle answers, sounds and signs being transmitted from a secret chamber above the shrine where a priest is hidden away, manipulating the god's wagging head with chains. One can still crawl into the hidden chamber today.

Alexander leaves the oracle of Siwa a god bent on world-conquest. If he is a god, though, he is one who will die at the age of thirty-three in Babylon, after a prolonged drinking bout and a fever. His closest companions and generals wait at his bedside to hear who will be named the successor.

The dying man does not name any one of them, however—for his answer is like that of an oracle.

"To the strongest! Kratisto!" he whispers. (One desperate general tries to claim he has pronounced "Craterus," his name.)

This answer sets their ambitious blood afire. His generals are strong, but none is *the strongest:* none can wrest world-empire for himself alone, though each will try in the following years. Thus Alexander's legacy is divided, with Ptolemy seizing Egypt and becoming the first of a Greek line that will end some three hundred years later with the famous Cleopatra, the seventh of her name.

She is a worthy conclusion to her dynasty: brilliant, beautiful and unscrupulous—a true Ptolemy who marries and murders both her younger brothers, as is not generally remembered, besides seducing Julius Caesar. Then, after his assassination, she backs the wrong Roman, doomed

Antony, with whom she finally, genuinely, seems to have fallen in love.

But if she is a Ptolemy, she introduces an innovation: She is the first and last to have learned Egyptian. This is not for official use, but as an intellectual diversion: She knows half a dozen other languages besides. We find her in the Talmud, of all places, asking Rabbi Meir, in Aramaic, how God occupies His time.

Thus Cleopatra's Greek gives way to Caesar's Latin. Egypt will never again speak its own language, a fact which reflects her new condition better than any other. Her gods become mongrels: part Egyptian, part Greek, part whatever flotsam and jetsam washes onto Alexandria's shores.

Her age-old mysticism will mingle first of all with Greek thought. Her people will live under Roman law, even coming to worship a Roman Emperor's eunuch-lover, Antinoöus. The beautiful boy drowns himself in the Nile, a mystical suicide-sacrifice to prolong the emperor Hadrian's life.

But this is just the beginning. For when the Roman empire becomes Christian, Egypt becomes Christian. And when the Roman empire splits, Egypt falls to its eastern half. Her peasants pray before Byzantine icons for over three hundred years—Christian monasticism will have its beginnings in Egypt. Then, except for stubborn monks practicing unimaginable feats of asceticism in the desert—stylites living exposed on pillars for twenty years at a time—Christ will be forgotten and Egypt will learn to pray—in Arabic—facing Mecca (in the seventh century, AD).

Throughout the nineteenth century, her intelligentsia is educated in France and into modern times, Egypt will be ruled by a dynasty of kings—*Khedives,* to give them their proper (Persian) title—who speak only Turkish or French, or English, but certainly not Arabic. That last avatar of ancient Egyptian, Coptic, survives only in a ritual form in the Egyptian Christian liturgy. Finally, in the 1960s, the last of the *Khedives,* the four-hundred-pound King Farouk, dies in exile in a Naples restaurant, surrounded by movie starlets, drinking the blood of twenty pairs of pigeons as an aphrodisiac, and calling out in Italian for oysters.

Between that strangled, gluttonous cry and Alexander the Great's pronouncement, *To the strongest!* lie two thousand years and a babble of languages echoing all the way back to the Greek carved on the Rosetta stone. This is the real prize of Napoleon's invasion of Egypt, this paean of praise for Ptolemy V Ephiphanes "Who pardoned those who had been arrested and who were in prison, and every person who had committed whatever crime long ago; Who gave grain to the god-houses yearly; Who took care to send infantry and cavalry and ships to drive back those who came to fight against Egypt from the sea coast as well as from the Great Green . . ." This near-miraculous find will help open the way to the decipherment. When the British triumph over the pathetic, dwindling troops Napoleon has left to languish in Egypt, they demand the stone as part of the French surrender.

General Menou will not agree to this. Negotiating the surrender, he gives in to almost all their terms except the "theft" of the stone. Day after day, week after week, he uses all kinds of ruses and stratagems to retain it: hiding it, denying its existence, even insisting that it is his "personal property." When he finally fails, he weeps openly as he hands it over. The French soldiers bitterly curse and swear at the victors carting it away. At every moment, a British officer reports, he fears that they will be attacked.

This is not the end of the matter: The inscriptions on the stone have been copied. Its gray surface has been covered with boot black (for lack of printer's ink) and pressed onto sheets of paper: the emperor's gift to the linguist.

The British may have the stone. On the side of it they arrogantly chisel the date and the fact of their victory. Theirs, however, is a victory that will be snatched away. This is the linguist's gift to the emperor: for when twenty-three years later, after twenty-three years of unremitting toil, Champollion finally succeeds in its decipherment, he will reclaim its glory for France.

True, by then it is a gift to a dead man, to an emperor who had perished on a small, barren island; to an ex-general whose body is laid naked on a billiard table and eviscerated as a hurried autopsy is performed.

Like the copies made of the stone, a death mask is made of the Emperor's face: a plaster impression of his features. That famous silhouette—through the memories and ideals it conjures—will continue to command.

Chapter Seven

Deliciae Alexandriae—
The Delights of Alexandria*

Prefatory Note

*THUS GOES THE proverbial Latin phrase which distinguishes these pleasures from the grosser ones of Rome. For the delights of Alexandria—in which the sensual *and* the intellectual *and* the aesthetic *and* the mystical intermingle!—can never surfeit or weary.

Rome's patricians, restless and nihilistic, became tired of their orgies and feasts and spectacles, the cruel gladiatorial contests where between fights, during intermissions, scores of criminals, captives, or slaves have their throats slit.

What do you do, after this, for an encore? Perhaps you arrange for a sensational reversal, a game where the gladiators turn on the audience, hurling their spears into the crowd in a prearranged stunt—a successful ruse, the "producer" is greatly applauded. But still there lurks the specter of boredom: for sensation repeated is as stale as yesterday's joke.

Even Rome's emperors sigh for the *deliciae Alexandriae.* Caesar spends his time in the city debating in its famed Museum, Cleopatra at his side. Hadrian can find no fitter memorial for his beloved eunuch-lover Antinoöus than making him a god here. And Nero consoles himself with the thought that were he ever deposed, he can become a singer on the stages of Alexandria.

In Alexandria one can enjoy the best of both the intellectual and the physical. Dinner parties take place in pools where the guests, immersed up to their chests in perfumed waters, sample exotic dishes on floating tables, listen to music, delight in neo-Platonic debate and watch theatrical events.

Greek thought mixes with exotic Hebrew and Egyptian wisdom. The Bible first appears in Greek in Alexandria, called the Septuagint, named for its seventy translators. Actors are admitted to the floating tables after performing scenes from the latest dramas and comedies. Comedies are especially suited to the Alexandrine nature, its culture being arch and sophisticated, taking pleasure, above all, in the bon mot, the mock epic, the epigram.

If Alexandria's intellectual pursuits are serious—mathematics, philosophy, astronomy, geography, history—its art is often trivial. The intellect is supreme in Alexandria, not the imaginative or emotional faculties.

The new comedy is imported and becomes all the rage. The Greek Menander ("O life! O Menander! Which is real?" the Alexandrine poet Callimachus cries) and the Latin Terence win applause. Tragic motifs are forgotten in the laughter of a "hit" such as *The Eunuch:* a younger brother, in love with his older brother's whore's serving girl, pretends to be a eunuch to gain admission to the whorehouse. He waits on the girl—in a state of prolonged erotic desire—bathing her, dressing her, etc. Can the serious political comedy of Aristophanes—work from a different time, a different place, a different consciousness—or the tragedies of Sophocles or Euripides hope to compete?

Ptolemy II knows his people. They don't want military triumphs such as Rome's, they take no delight in cruel, gladiatorial sport. When he arranges a spectacle, it is an artful one: the god of wine, Dionysus, is carried on a huge float, a panther skin around his shoulder, grapes in his hair; jeweled crowns, fantastic creations. The artifice and wealth of the city are put on display. *This* is the milieu of Alexandria.

By the time of Napoleon's conquest, this splendor is gone.

Alexandria's laughter has changed to the long Islamic cry, calling the faithful to prayer.

Its great lighthouse has toppled into the sea.

Its palaces and theaters have vanished without a trace.

⊓ ⊓ ⊓

"IT IS EASIER to understand humanity in general than to understand a single human being," La Rochefoucauld tells us—a maxim which perfectly applies to Napoleon. For the role *General* Bonaparte or *Emperor* Napoleon plays on the world stage is indeed much easier to understand than the demonic impulses and obsessions which thrust him onto that stage.

But if one truth about Napoleon the man is more striking than any other, it is this: History forms the air he breathes, the food he eats. Its examples, its ironies, its personalities form him. They are the medium through which he experiences reality.

He gazes at himself in the mirror and sees Caesar and Charlemagne and a hundred others. Even in defeat, he is Gustavus and Hannibal and Frederick Barbarossa. ("I appeal to you," he writes to the British after Waterloo, "as Themistocles appealed to his enemies.") He is Coriolanus and Alexander the Great not only on the battlefield, but even in the boudoir, even in affairs of the heart.

During the campaign in Egypt, Josephine is free of his oppressive presence and she no longer has to cancel assignations. ("Forgive me. I can't come tonight. Bonaparte will be home.") She abandons all caution and is seen everywhere with the charming Hippolyte Charles who knows how to tie his cravat so magnificently and whose jokes about Napoleon are repeated everywhere (like Napoleon, he is some eight years younger than Josephine).

But what she does not take into account is the entire Bonaparte clan. They hate her. His brothers and sisters and his mother have remained in France and are watching out for the family's honor in true Italian style . . . though, finally, it is from a friend that he will learn of the scandal.

When he does, he weeps and rages. For a while, he is almost out of his mind with grief. He clutches Josephine's sixteen-year-old son to him, whom he has made an aide-de-camp, ranting through the night to him about his beautiful, mercenary, sensual, faithless mother whose heavy rose perfume he always disliked and whose simplest gesture displayed more grace than that of any other woman he had ever known.

Cursing Josephine and her lover and love itself, he writes a despairing letter to his brother declaring that life no longer has meaning for him. "My passion for glory is gone. I am sick of humanity. I have no more reason to live. At twenty-nine years of age, I am worn out." The letter is intercepted on the Mediterranean by the British and published in the London newspapers.

While it arouses spiteful laughter from one end of Europe to the other, it is impossible to read it without feeling his pain. It is as far from a "literary" letter as it is possible to be: the unpremeditated *cri du coeur* of a man who will never again be romantically vulnerable. Women will be told to be in his bed, undressed, by such and such an hour when he will either appear or not, depending on his mood.

At this moment, though, he resembles nothing more than one of the crucified cupids in some Roman temple to Isis. At this moment, he cannot imagine the future or see himself ever reconciled to Josephine. He cannot conceive of the future Napoleon who will eagerly drag Josephine's successor to his bed, an eighteen-year-old Austrian archduchess, sleeping with her even before the marriage ceremonies. At this moment he would be shocked by the Emperor Napoleon-to-be who will dress up as a maid and playfully serve the famous Parisian courtesan Mademoiselle George breakfast after a night of pleasure. Now the innocence and devotion of the Polish beauty Countess Walewska is unthought of. At this moment when his heart is breaking, what is the metaphor which comes to his mind? Troy! "It is Troy again . . ." In the depths of despair—

Agamemnon!—in the outpouring of his disillusion, he invokes ancient warriors returning to faithless wives.

For him, these figures from history are desert mirages: approached too closely, they recede and finally disappear, leaving their pursuer clutching the air. How much of what Napoleon sees in them is what he wants to see, what he needs to see? For what are they, these historical names that give him strength, that form and console and inspire and in the end destroy him?

This Napoleon cannot allow himself to ask as he marches toward Alexandria on that stormy night in July— no more than Alexander the Great, that other young conqueror of Egypt, whose example obsessed Napoleon during the Egyptian campaign, could allow it to be asked two thousand years before. For during a furious drunken argument, when one of Alexander's companions, Clitus, a man who had fought side by side with Alexander through many battles (even having saved Alexander's life), shouts out damning words as friends tried to drag him away: "Kings steal the glory won by the blood of others!," a line from Euripides, Alexander runs him through with his sword.

It is a revealing moment in the psychological transformation of a "man of destiny" from any age, Alexander's, Napoleon's, or our own. And though one death more or less in the great struggle for the conquest of the world would not seem to matter so very much in the vast ebb and flow of history, the ancient historians (Arrian and Plutarch and Kleitarchos and Curtius) all dwell on it. It signals a crisis. It is the moment when Alexander is changed from what he was previously.

Gone is the Alexander who had reproached his court poet for boiling eels during the campaign—"Do you think, Cleisthenes, that Homer boiled eels while Agamemnon performed his great deeds?"—and who could laugh at the answer: "And do you think, O King, that Agamemnon looked into Homer's tent to see whether he boiled eels?"

After Egypt, Alexander is for better and for worse, a god, troubled only by his need for sleep and sexual intercourse—both of which, he said, reminded him of death.

Even in the days of its degradation, this divinity is felt in the city Alexander founds on the shores of the Mediterranean. As dawn breaks over the desert and Napoleon and his savants approach the ancient port they are filled with a sense of momentousness, of historical gravity, even though the Alexandria which had once dazzled the world is no longer there.

Decayed and dusty, it is barely a city, its population decimated by yearly outbreaks of the plague and famine, now numbering less than seven thousand souls. Two thousand years earlier, three hundred thousand lived in the city proper and another seven hundred thousand in the area outside its walls. Its unpaved streets are strewn with filth and roamed by beggars and barefoot street urchins. Its palaces, libraries, temples have vanished. Even their ruins are gone, the very stones sunk beneath the earth or carted away. This Alexandria greets Napoleon's eye.

The Mamelukes have left the port to fend for itself, instead making Cairo their base. It is not a regular army the French face when they arrive, but a crowd of ragged, desperate men, women, and children who look down on them from the city's only defense: ancient stone walls, weakened by time and neglect, though still rising forty feet.

There is a long prologue to the assault. While Napoleon takes his time disposing his troops, crying kites circle overhead and the sun emerges in its full force, driving the weary and hungry soldiers wild with thirst. This will be a continual torment during the campaign that follows. The scorching heat is made worse by the fact that it is the season when the *khamsin* begins to blow—a strong, hot wind that sweeps in from the desert, darkening the skies with a haze of burning sand.

General Kléber, a rough, plainspoken professional soldier in his fifties, a man who is vigorous and strong, is sent with his division to the north of the city, facing Pompey's Gate. Though now he is a "citizen" general, fighting in the name of the republic, he had earlier fought for Louis XVI and, before that, in the Austrian army for Marie-Thérèse: To him it is all the same. There is no love lost between him and Napoleon, whom he publicly refers to as "the little bugger," whose mistakes he is quick to catalogue and whose romantic vision of glory he scorns. Napoleon overlooks this insolence since he needs the man.

Opposite Kléber's troops, General Menou's division takes up its position in the west. An ex-aristocrat, well educated, emotional, and high-strung, Menou is softer than Kléber, both physically and emotionally. He is also less competent. Though he too dislikes Bonaparte, he is loyal. Napoleon knows he can count on him.

Finally, there is corpulent General Bon, deliberate in his actions. In the past he has been criticized for being too slow. Bon's division draws up to the east of the city, at the Rosetta Gate, that is, facing the direction of Rosetta, a second port some thirty miles away. Devoted to the pleasures of the table, Bon is, despite his appearance, a fearless soldier. He will stick to Napoleon throughout the eastern campaign, finally losing his life at Acre as he hurls himself into the thick of battle to stop a French retreat. Because of his size, he especially suffers from the heat. But for all his impatience to have done with the assault, he waits until Napoleon is ready.

On Napoleon's orders a messenger approaches the city walls with a flag of truce and offers safety in exchange for surrender. The people laugh and jeer and pelt him with filth.

Undiscouraged, Napoleon orders the messenger to return and try again. This time he is met with a volley of gunfire. General Bon has the bugles sounded and the soldiers, to the "terrifying shrieks and cries coming from the walls" as an officer, Savary, will write later, rush forward into the hail of rocks and gunfire.

Within the first moments of the uneven battle, two French major generals are seriously wounded—an anomaly in French military history. A well-aimed rock hurled from the walls fells General Menou (whose soldiers surround and protect him), while General Kléber, directing operations at the base of the walls, is shot in the head and carried off the field.

The soldiers manage to scale the high walls and beat back the defenders, a mixed mob with more spirit than strategy. Another military history anomaly: French soldiers battling veiled women who wield knives and throw rocks with deadly aim. Still, it is not long before the defenders, outnumbered and outfought, flee in disorder to a medieval fort in the heart of the city—the thin strip of land dividing the eastern harbor from the western.

The fort holds out for that entire day, as Napoleon watches from a nearby height, giving orders and sucking on oranges, since no water can be found. Finally, as the moon rises over the sea, a group of soldiers use the beams from a ship as a battering ram and manage to breach the walls of the fort. Some defenders escape to sea on a fishing vessel, while the remainder are taken prisoner.

The battle continues underground: In the catacombs where, in antiquity, Alexander's Greeks buried their dead, there is fierce fighting beside the sphinxes and winged gods. And in the ancient cisterns as well—a vast underground labyrinth used to collect rainwater. Beams of light shine through the deep shafts and from time to time dispel the shadows where men hide up to their waists in water, ready to die if only they can bring down an infidel with them—a desperate struggle that ends in a French victory.

The governor of the city surrenders, and Napoleon announces that the occupation of Alexandria will be a benevolent one. He hopes that the entire nation will hear of his magnanimity. He wants the people to rise up against the Mamelukes and welcome him as a liberator.

Despite his proclamations, there are violent incidents throughout that day and the next. As a soldier, Private Millet, recalls: "We thought that the city had surrendered when suddenly a volley of musketry was fired at us as we were passing by a mosque. A general who happened to be there [Adjutant General Boyer of the general staff] ordered us to force the gate and to spare no one we found inside. Men, women, and children were bayoneted."

It is a brutal measure. Though Napoleon has not ordered

it directly, he will take such measures again and again against the enemy, against his own soldiers in Europe, but especially here in Egypt where he seeks to dominate a country of two and a half million with thirty-eight thousand soldiers.

Are diseased prostitutes endangering the health of his troops? Sew them into sacks and throw them into the Nile—at least a few to serve as a warning!

Has a French doctor refused to treat plague-ridden soldiers? Dress him in a woman's clothes and parade him through the streets. This causes a Frenchwoman, resenting the slur on her sex, to challenge Napoleon to a duel.

When an Egyptian woman is raped and murdered, two French soldiers seen nearby are executed without trial. Are they innocent? It turns out they are indeed. Well, they are martyrs in the great cause of order.

In his youth, Napoleon saw frenzied crowds break into Versailles and massacre the king's Swiss guards, reverting to barbarism that would revolt the most hardened. He never forgot the spectacle of the unrestrained mob. If his orders are cruel, he would shrug, the cruelty is not wanton but in keeping with military and political necessity as he perceives them. In such matters, only severity succeeds, and for Napoleon success is the ultimate good.

There are two dangers in considering such acts in the

twenty-first century. The first is not putting Napoleon in his nineteenth century context, in the heroic historical tradition in which he saw himself.

That is, of forgetting that Beethoven dedicated the *Eroica* to Napoleon in an outpouring of admiration (a dedication he "retracted" for political not moral reasons—being incensed on learning that Napoleon had proclaimed himself emperor); of forgetting that for Goethe, Napoleon's spell was never broken; that for Hegel, Napoleon was *the* spirit of the times and that, for the youth of the nineteenth century, Napoleon was the supreme example of the heroic and the sublime.

They saw in Napoleon not the man who could order prostitutes sewn into a sack but the patron of the arts and sciences, the reformer who preferred merit over birth, the Prometheus struggling to create a new world order. He is the conqueror who gallops through the desert, ascertaining the practicability of reviving a canal built by the pharaohs as one of his many measures to revitalize the desperately poor, oppressed, stagnant land. This canal would finally be built later on in the century by a Frenchman and with French finance; for Napoleon's ideas will forever leave their mark on Egypt. In fact, it is especially after the French leave that the full force of his influence is felt.

It is generally reported in contemporary accounts, in the *Courier d'Egypte,* for example, the newspaper established by the French in Egypt, that when the Rosetta stone was discovered, when a soldier, swinging his pickax, hit against something hard—a stone covered with writing in both Egyptian and Greek—"the significance of the find was immediately recognized."

But if this was so, if the men toiling in the heat and the dust did not simply ignore the heavy stone with its curious writing—it weighed three quarters of a ton—if they did not simply seek to finish up their work and seize whatever pleasures they could find, that was because of one man, Napoleon Bonaparte, who had from the first insisted on the dual purpose of this conquest: learning as well as power. And his exhortations had so permeated the consciousness of the entire French force—from the most distinguished savant to the youngest drummer boy—as to make the discovery of the stone an event of wonder among the men.

Could the men who came after Napoleon have inspired that? The dull, gouty Louis XVIII, placed on the throne by France's enemies? Or the brother who followed, Charles X, a man with even fewer ideas, a small, vengeful spirit, and a passion only for court etiquette?

Yet still there are the *crimes*—there is no other name for them: a long, long list. Goya's painting *The Second of May* is by itself enough to make one feel their horror and inhumanity: the immediacy of the scene Goya paints, the beauty and innocence of the faces, the wild-eyed yearning for life of the victims standing before French executioners. Once you see Napoleon's victims, it is impossible to forget them.

When that other great French statesmen, Cardinal Richelieu, died a century earlier, the pope at that time, a Barberini, Urban VIII, remarked while crossing himself: "If there is a God, Richelieu has much to answer for. But if not—*if not*—" he shrugged with a smile, "then he led a successful life."

Napoleon was too much of a romantic to be content with such a cynical epitaph, with such acceptance of the world as it is. He might sometimes affect a world-weary pose, but it does not encompass the full complexity of the man. He strove, always, from first to last, to re-create the world: to impose a glorious ideal on a resisting humanity! If he was cruel, it was the cruelty of idealism.

No, Pope Urban's epitaph did not fit him, he would have insisted, throwing his great achievements onto the scales, balancing them against the crimes and barbarities of war. This is the second danger in considering Napoleon: placing him in the heroic historical tradition in which he saw himself, ignoring the old saw: *Never take a man at his own valuation.*

Napoleon had himself portrayed in a hundred different romantic paintings. In one, he crosses the Alps on a magnificent white horse instead of the donkey we know he rode and from which, moreover, we know he slipped more than once. Just so, he would have conjured up the words of one romantic poet or another to excuse his terrible crimes. Can much suffering be laid to his door? Well, then, "the cut worm forgives the plow."

It is a defense, indeed.

But *caveat emptor!* Let the buyer beware! For as La Rochefoucauld reminds us: "Language was given to human beings that they might conceal their thoughts from others."

And even from themselves, we might add, especially when talking of that sacred monster, Napoleon Bonaparte.

ON THE SECOND day of Napoleon's occupation of Alexandria, the public baths are closed so that the French soldiers might do their laundry. They crowd into the crumbling building raised three centuries before as an act of piety. Beneath Quait Bey's high medieval domes, under carved arches, cusped and foliate and stalactiform, the Frenchmen toss their lice-ridden clothes into huge boiling cauldrons, their cursing and laughter echoing off the stone walls.

Among the many sketches by the artist Denon is one of the medieval bathhouse. He also draws the sagging quays of the harbor, and the shuttered houses of the deserted streets. He even manages to capture "the universal silence and sadness" that he writes about in his journal.

As always, he is conscientious and hardworking when recording what he sees. For as an artist Denon has the technique that may be acquired in an academy, but none of the inspiration which cannot be taught. At fifty-one, he is a brilliant dilettante with a talent for living and an ability to laugh at fortune and its reversals.

In his youth, he had aspired to be a diplomat and was attached to the French embassy first in Switzerland, then Italy, then Russia. His good looks and charm caught the attention of Catherine the Great. Whether he also won the all-important approval of her "tester," Countess Bruce, is not recorded.

Denon is a playwright and a raconteur. His short story *Le Pointe de Lendemain* (*The Sting of the Morning After*) won Balzac's praise as "a school for married men." He is also something of a pornographer: the etchings in his *Oeuvre Priapique* can be called nothing else. His eroticism finally gets him into trouble: as a lover of Louis XV's mistress,

Madame Pompadour, he becomes the official caretaker of her antique gems. It is an appointment that would have cost Denon his life during the Terror, if the great artist David had not saved him.

The kindness is uncharacteristic of David. The politically astute David had managed to become not only a member of Robespierre's Committee of Public Safety but, for two weeks, its president. During this time he feverishly condemns everyone: fellow artists and former patrons alike. Over four hundred death sentences bearing David's signature survive, perhaps most tragically, one for the gifted young poet Andrea Chénier, who goes to the scaffold cursing the cruel artist.

It is a mystery then why David—the creator of severe, neoclassical paintings such as *The Lictors Bringing Brutus the Bodies of His Sons* and *The Oath of the Horatti,* examples of Roman courage meant to inspire the revolutionary youth—would stoop to save an artist such as Denon. A dilettante still working in the frivolous prerevolutionary fashion, Denon's ideals were *Cupid Stealing a Nightgown from a Sleeping Maiden* and *The Swing,* a painting in which a husband pushes his wife on a swing while her lover, hidden in the bushes, peeks up her skirts.

With a few cruel strokes of his pen, David is able to capture Marie Antoinette on the way to the guillotine: hands tied behind her, back straight, features ugly with suffering as she stares ahead with unseeing pride. The sketch is characteristic of David. If Denon had drawn it, it would have been his nature to choose the trivial moment just before Antoinette enters the executioner's tumbrel: to draw her as she calls for her favorite plum-colored shoes and squats to pee next to a wall. Such is the difference between the two artists.

For whatever reason, David saves Denon, having his name taken off the list of the expatriates, a euphemism for the condemned, and putting the artistic ex-lover of Madame Pompadour to work designing uniforms for the revolutionary guard.

This is done with Denon's usual verve and style. He has talent, though not genius. He never created great epic canvasses for Napoleon like David's, never achieved the daring of David's *The Death of Marat* or the intensity of David's self-portraits. Denon's self-portrait, though irresistible for its joie de vivre, is all surface. A lesser artist but a better man than David, Denon's achievement will be of a different kind.

During his stay in Egypt he will tirelessly, heroically produce thousands of accurate sketches under the most difficult circumstances, drawing unknown temples and forgotten ruins, recording wall after wall of hieroglyphs. These will be of crucial importance for the new discipline being born.

Accompanying the army six hundred miles into southern Egypt, he endures thirst, hunger, scorching heat, and the fatigue of forced marches—hardships which overcome many a younger man.

Undeterred by danger, time and again he will remain behind after his comrades leave to finish a drawing, sometimes escaping death by the skin of his teeth. The unevenness of one sketch, he explained, was due to a shoot-out with a marauder who had suddenly appeared in the desert. Another time, during one of the innumerable desert skirmishes, he risks his life to save that of a black child, mutilated and left to die on the steps of an ancient temple. He will adopt this boy and eventually bring him back to France.

Denon has courage and a devil-may-care attitude. The insouciance that brings him to Egypt in the first place then gets him into a hundred-and-one scrapes . . . starting from the very beginning, from that hot bright day in July (laundry day in the army) when, hearing that his ship, the *Juno,* is anchored offshore, he decides to row out and retrieve a change of clothes and his belongings.

Since soundings of the harbor have not yet been taken, a process requiring some two weeks, no one knows whether the water is deep enough to accommodate the heavy ships, so the fleet lies exposed at Abukir Bay, some twenty miles to the east. Denon sets out in search of the skiff or rowboat that he'll need, and perhaps a companion to go with him, first stopping off at headquarters to see what can be found.

All is chaos here. Napoleon, despite his phenomenal energy, is strained to the utmost. Not only is he organizing the occupation, but he is in the midst of preparing for his next step as well.

There will be a four-pronged march through the desert, the immediate occupation of Cairo as the goal. Eighteen thousand soldiers are to be set in motion before the end of the day. The last time the French were in Egypt, during the crusades, under Louis the Saint, the king waited before taking action, spending nine days immersed in prayer while he and his entire army were surrounded and taken captive. Napoleon—whose only prayers are a stream of curses—will not repeat Louis the Saint's mistake.

All arrangements for the march must be made immediately. Inconceivable speed is one of Napoleon's main strategic weapons. Where another commander would have taken basic precautions, collecting water for the march or sending out scouts, Napoleon saves time by calculating how many of the men will die of thirst and hunger, factoring into his calculations that a certain number will not have the strength to complete the march. What matters most is to get the army to Cairo before anyone could have thought it possible, to catch his enemies off guard, to surprise, to dismay—and then to crush them.

Denon stands at the edge of the whirlwind Napoleon has created, watching the constant coming and going. A mob has descended on headquarters, each man arguing that his mission is more urgent, his request more pressing than any other's.

In charge of the engineers, Monge is disputing with chief of staff Berthier over how the city's defenses should be strengthened. Desgennetes, in charge of the medical team, is insisting on decent arrangements for the wounded to anyone who will listen. Officers clamor for provisions for their hungry men. And local guides offer their services for the impending march through the desert, each giving conflicting accounts of the terrain which must be covered. The French do not yet have a single accurate and detailed map.

Sailors arrive with reports from Admiral Brueys who is worried about the safety of his ships. And aides-de-camp hurry to post the latest decrees throughout the city: the food prices Napoleon has fixed.

In the midst of everything else, Bonaparte has taken time to issue orders regarding how much Alexandria's merchants can charge for a pound of lentils or a fat goose. These prices the merchants will ignore, however, ironically asking for much less. For, they reason, when the Mamelukes cut the foreigners to bits—as everyone is sure they will—what will be the good of French coin? Instead of French money— the possession of which will be evidence of collaboration, after all—they want to be able to prove how many French- men they have killed, to be able to boast of their loyalty and courage when their masters return. And so they charge the soldiers the brass buttons from their uniforms—so-and-so many for a pound of lentils, and so many for a goose . . .

But what are these gloomy predictions, this whispering of the marketplace to Napoleon? He has spoken! He has decided what the price of lentils and geese, fat and lean, will be. The printing presses are unloaded from the ships right away—even before the medicine or dry biscuit. The price lists—the first words ever printed in Egypt—are plas- tered on walls and doorways . . . not far from the heroic dead who still lie where they fell, stripped of uniforms and gnawed by stray dogs.

Napoleon's idea of mummifying some for a future mili- tary museum is shouted down by the savants. In good time, they will be buried. But first Bonaparte must deal with imams and officials and shipowners and, perhaps most important of all, the Bedouin sheiks who have come to sell him desperately needed camels and horses. These devious men spend so much time haggling and disputing terms, it is as if they actually intend to deliver the animals they now promise.

In the midst of all this clamor and confusion, Denon sketches: the wizened, intriguing features of the Egyptian governor, who, ever since sighting the warships outside the harbor, spends all his time in attendance upon Bonaparte; the French engineers arguing over their plans; a soldier carrying dispatches, his jacket already missing some buttons.

By chance, the artist encounters a friend, a fellow savant. It is the young poet Perceval-Grandmaison who has just been put in charge of some requisitioned donkeys. Donkeys! Grandmaison seethes. Would they have put Shakespeare or Dante or Virgil in charge of donkeys? In the urgent press of affairs, Napoleon's imported savants have been called from their exalted speculations to perform whatever tasks are needed: running errands or compiling inventories or caring for the wounded—what's more, doing so on a private's meager rations.

Denon explains he is on his way to the *Juno* where Grandmaison has left his belongings as well. Abandoning the poor, uninspiring donkeys, the two wander together toward an outlying part of town as they look for a skiff to take them to their ship.

They never reach the *Juno.* Hours later, as the moon rises over Alexandria, the two Frenchman are lost, climbing over embankments, wading through water—still without fresh clothes or their belongings. They are pursued by what Denon in his memoirs calls "the 6th plague of Egypt": packs of wild, hungry dogs who snarl at the poet and painter. Finally Denon, ex-lover of Madame Pompadour and future director of the Louvre, is reduced to hurling rocks at them and cursing. Grandmaison has fallen into a ditch and twisted his ankle, making it difficult for him to walk.

Denon is a good friend of Grandmaison's. The two argued and talked throughout the entire crossing on the *Juno.* Now, however, stranded on menacing, dark shores, he is somehow less interested in meter and rhyme.

Sounds of gunshots and sporadic fighting can be heard throughout the night. The population is still hostile. No one believes that Napoleon has come to free Egypt, to liberate her from Mameluke oppression. His propaganda and proclamations are scoffed at, while the pronouncements of Al-Azhar's sheiks—who have also been busy with propaganda—command respect. They stir up bands of vigilantes who roam the countryside, attacking any French they meet while giving refuge to the Mamelukes who had so cruelly ruled over them.

For the Mamelukes are believers. Cruel or not, foreign or not, speakers of Turkish or Albanian or some other tongue, blue-eyed and blond from the Caucasus or black from Nubia, the Mamelukes acknowledge God and his prophet Mohammed.

True, they have no heirs and so each regime change is fraught with quarrels and bloodshed. Yet the exquisite tombs and mosques and caravanserais they build—with their delicate arabesques and plays of light and shadow and masterpieces of carved calligraphy—are the pride of the land.

And these Frenchmen? Godless, shameless, uncircumcised, they are drinkers of whiskey and wine. Unsatisfied with boys, they make love to respectable, veiled women.

In a word: infidels.

And in another: dogs.

Thus Denon and Grandmaison pass half the night in danger of their lives, sitting talking by the seashore and hoping that a French patrol will come by—as one eventually does—to lead them to safety.

Chapter Eight

ⲔⲒⲨⲎ*

1806 Summer. France.
Vif—in the mountains outside the village.

IT IS IMPOSSIBLE to see the sun set in Grenoble.
It sinks behind the snow-capped mountains surrounding
the city. Suddenly, it is night.

But on the mountains, high up over a lonely valley, every
shade of the fading day is as distinct as a note of music.
Here a swarthy, foreign-looking youth—Jean François—
stands alone, watching eagles soar and circle overhead.

Shadows fall over the pine and beech tree forest where

---

* Coptic. From a second-century AD papyrus scroll. The word cried out by a
possessed man, hung up in church.
                          Meaning unknown.

he has spent the day wandering. Soon the naked crags and peaks are plunged into darkness along with the winding paths that lead up to them—narrow paths used only by goatherds and smugglers and, on that summer's day, by a young man with a thousand ancient words running in his head. They echo more loudly than the locusts chirring in the valley below.

It has been a strenuous day, but Jean François needs to climb and climb and forget the petty humiliations of his schoolmasters and the frustrations of the past year, his last in the *lycée*. Scrambling over fallen trees and huge boulders, he comes to a woodcutter's shack where he spends the night. Jotting down all he has seen and thought, he composes enthusiastic, though not very good, poetry inspired by youth and first love.

For Jean François is in love; and, moreover, with a woman who speaks only French! Some six years older than he, she has something of the pallor and ethereal look of a consumptive.

Her name is Pauline Berriat. Her sister Zoé has just married his brother Jacques. The two are thrown together, Pauline and Jean François—still shy with women—not only in Grenoble but during the long, idyllic summer in the mountains where he is staying with his brother and where Pauline comes to visit.

As a match it is impossible. Pauline Berriat is the daughter of a prosperous lawyer, and he has only slowly, reluctantly, become reconciled to the idea of one daughter marrying a scholar—though a scholar "with prospects" as Jacques is said to have. Monsieur Berriat has no intention of allowing his second daughter to become involved with another scholar—who has none.

After all, Jacques has been admitted to the learned society of Grenoble, the Académie delphinale: a great honor for anyone and an unprecedented tribute for someone like Jacques, who has no degrees or formal training. In addition, Jacques has supporters, influential men in the Académie who are bent on helping him survive. They see to it that he is made Grenoble's librarian and then secure an appointment for him in the university.

But more is involved in Berriat's decision than such objective facts. What is decisive, what distinguishes Jacques from Jean François in the prudent lawyer's eyes are trifles: a gesture, a tone of voice, what is not said more than what is said. It is nothing, really: but *everything,* all the imponderables which make up a first and never-to-be-effaced impression.

For Jean François is an enthusiast with an abrupt, nervous manner who listens to Pauline's father without really listening, who "comes to life" in a drawing room only when the most preposterous (to Berriat's mind) questions are discussed, who sometimes bites his lips till they bleed when an idea strikes him and who is given to fainting.

No, these are more decisive factors than objective prospects. What wins Jacques his bride is the way that (unlike Jean François) he can deal with many different kinds of people. Jacques is discreet, political, sober, worldly wise. It is one thing to be able to endure poverty (as Jean François will). It is quite another to perform a clerk's duties for five years running as Jacques has (and as Jean François never could): patiently taking care of business details while acquiring a breadth of learning that will win him the admiration of the Académie delphinale.

Jean François, no matter what he argues, what he promises to achieve, stands no chance with Berriat. Zoé tries to explain this to her new brother-in-law, consoling Jean François with a combination of sympathy, bourgeois indignation, and teasing banter.

A clever woman, she is a good wife to Jacques, kind to Jean François from their first meeting when she draws him out with intelligent questions about his studies. Hearing how much he loves Arabic, she has him translate his nickname, Cadet, into Arabic: *Seghir*. This becomes the name Jean Francois' friends and family use for him from this time on and how he signs his letters. *Seghir*, Cadet: "younger brother"—like the name he will use in his publications later, Champollion *jeune,* Champollion the younger.

It is not only a mark of his deference for Jacques, of his deep respect for his brother, but a sign of how he sees himself. Jacques' faith in him will always be the source of Jean François' own belief in himself. If the world is indifferent, hostile, and mocking, Jacques' support for his impulsive, tempestuous younger brother is unwavering. And more: Jacques has demonstrated, by his example, what toil and determination can achieve.

But though Jacques' presence is a vital and almost an overwhelming one for his brother, Jean François' beloved, Pauline, remains a cipher, a mere shadow. She walks by Jean François' side in the mountains; meets him secretly in Grenoble; or sees him at her sister's house, where she plays the piano or recites poetry for him in her languid way. Of her interest in his work, or of a willingness to defy her father, we know not a word. Yet she remains loyal and faithful to Jean François even after he leaves Grenoble to study in Paris.

Time goes by, a year, then another. His letters to her dwindle in number. Pauline is forgotten and Jean François lives in a small room in Paris alone with the hieroglyphs: his real mistress, the beautiful, inscrutable writing. And if his passion for her is like a disease, it is a disease that gives his life meaning.

☐ ☐ ☐

IT SEEMS AS if Jean François passes from childhood to manhood in an instant. There are all the recognizable, universal moments of youth . . .

There is first love, perhaps felt all the more intensely given his passionate nature.

There is the friend: a fellow student named Joachim Wangehis who stands up for Jean François in the *lycée*. This makes the school authorities separate them. Writes Jean François to Jacques, "I am supposed to be a 'bad influence'! They warned him to stay away from me and he did not! He paid no attention to them. And so they have changed his schedule of classes. I will no longer see him. That's how they do things here!"

And there is *the crime*—a trip with Wangehis to see a forbidden "show"—images of the newly excavated ruins of Pompei projected in the *Laterna Magica*. Light is made to shine through scenes painted on glass and alternated quickly, one after the other, the illusion of motion accompanied by thunder and explosions from a "sound machine."

Innocent images, when all is said and done: a mother clutching her child, a beggar with his arm around a dog, priests buried under their toppled gods. There is not much to account for the scandal the display has caused except, perhaps, for the Roman lady caught in the gladiators' barracks when the volcano erupts, "sketched from life"— as the advertisement states, or rather "from death"—the woman in her gold bracelets and jewels preserved perfectly in the volcanic ash, two manacled gladiators at her side.

Love, friendship, rebellion; then "a certificate of study and conduct" from the *lycée*. At sixteen, Jean François is ready to face the world, which he does suddenly, by surprise, five days after his graduation.

With more brotherly pride than wisdom, Jacques has decided to risk his own reputation and Jean François' self-esteem, arranging for him to deliver a paper before the Académie delphinale. But why he should have chosen this particular setting for Jean François' debut is a mystery. Jacques knows the conservative, skeptical nature of the academy's membership, distinguished scholars and diplomats, scientists and mathematicians who are rigorous and critical and severe. Called away from their own work, they expect to be rewarded with discourse that is extraordinary. This is the raison d'etre of the Académie.

Jacques knows the idea of a young student presenting a paper here will astonish everyone. Regardless of what Jean François has to say, there is something to provoke ridicule simply in the fact of a sixteen-year-old lecturing established scholars, authorities in their respective fields. Jacques knows that a failure elsewhere could be shrugged off by his brother, but that here it will publicly humiliate Jean François. Yet Jacques goes ahead with the scheme.

There is a practical consideration, perhaps. Young men are being drafted daily, their ages younger and younger as Napoleon's soldiers die on battlefields and must be replaced. But if a success would help Jean François receive a military exemption, why here, precisely where success is hardest to achieve?

Later Jacques will say that he had followed the progress of his brother's ideas and decided that he was ready. Ready for what, though? Intense scrutiny of ideas which are just beginning to germinate? Examination of a judgment which is not yet mature? An ordeal?

It is true that by the time Jean François finishes at the *lycée,* he has already sketched out his plans for a work on Egypt, but this is an early attempt. Modestly giving it the title *Essay on the Geographical Description of Egypt Before the Conquest of Cambyses* (the Persian conquest), Jean François brings all his research to bear on a single question: the place names of ancient Egypt, its cities, rivers, oases, provinces . . .

Jacques feels the work is defensible. Actually, not only is the essay defensible, it reflects masterful scholarship, the control of an enormous amount of material woven into a coherent, thought-provoking whole.

Rather, it is an essay that would be defensible, if the

young Jean François remembers to stay within its limits, if he is careful not to improvise or get carried away—dangers against which Jacques has cautioned his brother. But try to preach discretion to an enthusiast. Tell a moth to avoid the flame or Icarus to be wary of the sun . . . Jacques is pissing against the wind.

And so, five days after his graduation, the young scholar appears at the Académie delphinale. He is introduced briefly—what is there to say about him, after all? Striding up to the podium, he begins to speak.

He is brilliant. In a tour de force, he analyzes scores of Arabic, Latin, Greek, and Coptic Egyptian place names; sometimes they are translations or paraphrases of older, pharaonic names; sometimes, more rarely, they contain elements of the original language (the Coptic names especially). These are sounds that have survived thousands of years since last spoken as part of the ancient, forgotten language. Distorted, changed, combined with other languages, missing letters, endings (phonetic decay)—they nevertheless provide hints and suggestions, which Jean François explores in speculative asides.

Taking a first step out of the charmed circle of the defensible, he continues on his dangerous path by predicting that whatever ancient Egyptian has survived in Coptic will provide an important clue in the decipherment of the hieroglyphs.

Of course it must be remembered, he continues—proceeding in the self-contradictory, dialectical way characteristic of all real thought—that from antiquity on, the hieroglyphs have been described as a silent, symbolic language: each image representing an idea, a word, an allegory. There are far too many hieroglyphs to represent an alphabet, far too many to represent sounds . . . hundreds (in Ptolemaic times, thousands). Yet Coptic words, Coptic sounds are and will be crucial. Just why and how this is, he does not yet know and cannot yet explain.

Jean François, though deep in his studies, is still far from tackling any of the new inscriptions brought back to Europe by Napoleon's savants, a wealth of writing, both papyri and statues and prolific copies made from vast temple walls and many-chambered tombs—Denon's the most important among them.

It is an embarrassment of riches, in addition to which—most tantalizing of all—there are the inscriptions on the Rosetta stone, the three scripts which have been studied unsuccessfully by linguists across Europe. In fact, the experienced authority Silvestre de Sacy, the decipherer of the Sassanid Persian inscriptions at Naqsh-i-Rustam, a man who will soon be one of Jacques' mentors in Paris, has opined that in the present state of knowledge, decipherment of the hieroglyphs is impossible.

Perhaps one day, perhaps by chance, de Sacy believes,

success will be achieved. But only by chance, only because of some lucky find, some fortuitous discovery that brings to light material not yet known. Until that time, declares this eminent professor of Persian and Arabic, this scholar well-versed in Coptic, the quest is futile.

This pronouncement Jean François completely rejects though he cannot yet say why. Seeing Jacques bury his face in his hands, he tries to circle back to the problem of *Shunet es Zebib*—the name for a fortress at Abydos meaning *Storehouse of Raisins* in Arabic. The same sounds appear in classical authors (predating the Arab conquest) and which must therefore . . . Mid-sentence Jean François stops. He has finished.

"I listened in the silence to my beating heart," he later remembers. The young linguist stands alone and exposed. He has no idea that, after the first shock of surprise is over, this silence will give way to loud acclaim. Or that in the next moment, surrounded by admirers, he will become the youngest member of the Académie delphinale.

ꌷ ꌷ ꌷ

TO PARIS! A truly wondrous city, since Napoleon has graced her with great art looted from all over Europe. From Germany and Italy and Austria, with Denon to advise him at his side, the Emperor brings back wagonloads of canvasses and antique sculpture to adorn his capital, which, nevertheless, is crowded, filthy, and foul-smelling! Napoleon has been too busy with world-conquest to concern himself with sewers. The Seine will do.

Nor has he repaired the destruction visited upon the city during the revolution: the royal monuments toppled by frenzied crowds and the great houses stripped bare. Though more than a decade has passed, rubble and charred buildings are still to be seen everywhere.

A few paces from Napoleon's imperial institutes, narrow, squalid streets turn in upon themselves in a dark labyrinth left over from medieval days. And it is precisely here that Jean François takes up residence. In a small, bare room facing a wall, he is now far from the mountains of Grenoble with their thin, white waterfalls, their wildflowers and pines.

His health is affected immediately perhaps because of the bad air, the stench, and the crowding, or perhaps because of his poverty. The little that Jacques can spare does not go far in Paris. Jean François develops a chronic cough and splitting headaches. He is given to shortness of breath and exhaustion. But despite the shock to his physical constitution, there is intellectual joy for Jean François here. At the College de France, the Special School of Oriental Languages, there are long hours of Chaldean and of Hebrew; of Arabic, Ethiopian, Coptic, and Persian.

His capacity for work is staggering, though work is not the word for it. He is insatiable, intoxicated, pursuing a course of study, a range of languages that would be difficult for several students, let alone one. And he arranges for private instruction. An Egyptian priest at the church of St. Roch tutors him in Coptic. A Turkish diplomat from the Porte converses with him in Arabic. And there is a collector of antiquities, an alluring French lady with a mellifluous voice who has traveled to the ends of the earth—and who is fortunately fluent in Persian.

The city opens a new world to him. Not only are there other linguists of great stature, such as Silvestre de Sacy and Louis-Mathieu Langlès and Prosper Audran, who has such respect for his student that he sometimes has him teach the Aramaic or Hebrew class himself, but there are the manuscripts as well: texts which would not have been available to Jean François.

There is a magnificent collection of incunabula in Paris: rare books brought back from Italy as spoils of war, crates and crates that Napoleon pillaged from the Vatican, along with countless works of art.

They arrive in a grand triumphal procession. The emperor boasts that he has made Paris the new Rome. To the rolling of drums and the booming of cannon, the priceless treasures enter the sewerless, victorious city, proudly displayed in ceremonial coaches which pause every few paces before the admiring crowds.

First come the paintings, canvasses covered with Madonnas and saints and popes (Caravaggio and Titian, Velázquez and Raphael)—a magnificent procession which, as Napoleon's police chief Fouché notes, is a godsend to the pickpockets working the crowd.

Next come the statues from antiquity, carried on litters by proud soldiers in resplendent uniforms. There are Greek and Roman gods and goddesses, the Apollo Belvedere and the nude Diana preparing for her bath; and human figures, like the *Spinaria,* the young boy taking a thorn from his foot, a first-century marble. And the *Laocoön* depicting the priest struck down as he warns his countrymen not to let the wooden horse enter Troy: Wrapped in the coils of a great serpent, he dies together with his two sons. Their sculpted agony is so dynamic, so filled with noble, anguished passion that spectators cry out in wonder at the sight of it, just as Michelangelo and Pope Julius had when it was unearthed three centuries before.

And, finally, the books appear, the most splendid displayed as dramatically as the works of art: fragile papyrus rolls preserved in cases of silver and gold; thick, parchment volumes covered with jewels.

Brought to the understaffed National Library, many works will remain uncatalogued and in their original crates for years, though on the recommendation of his teachers Jean François is given access to them. To his delight, he discovers many Coptic works, obscure texts abounding with strange words that deepen his knowledge of the language.

Written in the first and second and third centuries AD when Egypt's old beliefs were being transformed into the new, they are part Christian, part pagan; ecstatic prayers and crude spells and mystical speculation.

In language resonant with echoes of ancient Egyptian—for an ear straining to hear them—they tell how a demonic spirit, the Archon Sabaoth, challenges the great mystery of Light. Or they recount a simple story: A desert monk, returning to his cave, begs a snake he has disturbed not to slither away, vowing to abandon his home if the creature leaves him.

Or—on a small scrap of papyrus cut into the shape of a dagger—the ancients utter enchantments. *Tartari! Saro! Pthah!* a man calls on the gods (degraded gods, by the second Christian century: mere demiurges and demons) *Astabias! I am that which raised Judas against Ei, Jesus until he was crucified upon the wood. I am that which went up to heaven calling out, Eloi Ei Elemas. I myself am god. As for me, then, I beg . . . put hatred and separation between Sipa son of Siheau and Ouartheihla, daughter of Cauhare* (Louvre E.14.250). *Make his [member] like a rag on a dung heap, like an ant frozen in winter! Let her hunger for me like a bitch for a dog, like a sow for a boar . . .*

God is absolutely alone, begins another text of heretical, Christian Egypt. Not even St. Mark, whose blackened, mummified body will be smuggled out of Egypt in a barrel of pickled pork when Islam arrives centuries later—not even St. Mark can woo daring, imaginative, speculative, superstitious, stubborn Egypt from its many heresies, its Monophysitism, its Gnosticism, its unnameable beliefs tracing back, in one way or another, to the repressed memory of its dead yet living gods. *God is unknowable and separate from every created being. The son of god . . . a created being and so not god in the full sense . . . But may He not be worshipped as a lesser deity?—May He not be*—The work goes on for many chapters, its Coptic words and sounds studied, recorded, hoarded by Jean François.

Obscure and difficult—*Akhnoui Akham Abra Aabaoth, Akg'hag'ha is my name, Sabagha is my true name, Glot the might is my name*—these studies will bear fruit though their usefulness in deciphering the hieroglyphs is not immediately apparent, either to Jean François or to his mentors.

But, as Terence Duquesne, another brilliant Coptic scholar, will observe in the twentieth century, the inscrutable names and esoteric words in such texts are like the chalk marks left by Gypsies: marks that point the way to fellow wanderers, but which are meaningless to others.

Jean François is just such a "wanderer"; he approaches his goal—the hieroglyphs on the Rosetta stone—indirectly, ranging far and wide, by instinct, waiting to attack them until he has learned all that he can.

Years later, when Napoleon's stolen books find their way back to the Vatican library, the scholar Sir William Gell will relate, "I think there are few Coptic books in Europe he [Champollion] has not examined. A friend of mine told me there is no book in the Vatican in that language, that has not remarks of Champollion in almost every page, which he made when the manuscripts were at Paris."

Jean François devotes himself especially to his Coptic although, after all, what is it? A patois, a jargon written in Greek letters, a jumble of words spoken by a people who, conquered again and again, had forgotten not only the classical form of their language but even their own script. Moreover, a patois that has itself gone out of use a thousand years before Jean François takes up its study!

Replaced by Arabic after the Arab conquest, Coptic becomes an echo of an echo, a memory of a memory: a vernacular, a slang, a debased language gradually dying into

silence. Its tones, inflections, its expressions are all reduced
to a fixed liturgy of "corrupted" words and a few crates of
books in the National Library—books looted by a visionary general and pored over night after night by a feverish
boy!

His theory that Coptic still bears some affinity to ancient
Egyptian is still an unproven theory, little more than a
guess, as Jean François knows. And even supposing that it is
a remote descendant of the ancient language, how changed
it must be—another problem. How many centuries separate Coptic from ancient Egyptian—and how many foreign conquests, how many foreign words and sounds and
scripts have been interposed between the two.

Still Jean François persists in his study, going through
crate after unopened crate, cutting through twine and
breaking the military seals affixed in Rome. Reading
through the night, his voice echoes in the empty library, for
he reads out loud, a habit picked up from the ancients for
whom the written word was not silent but filled with
sound.

He reads: ⲟⲩⲁϩⲙⲉⲕ ⲉⲣⲟⲟⲩ ⲉⲕⲱϣ ⲉⲃⲟⲗ *They will awake*
. . . the strange Coptic words wrapped in their ill-fitting
Greek shroud whose alphabet can only express just so
much (but not all) of the ancient language, so that seven
letters must be added to the Greek ones. Seven letters
modeled on the hieroglyphs in a simplified form, almost

unrecognizable as such, it is true, but letters through which ancient Egyptian struggles—like the arms of the mummified god Osiris—to break through its cerements and winding bands . . . the *shei* ϣ, the *fei* ϥ, the *khei* ϧ, the *tjima* ϭ, the *djiandjia* ϫ, the *tei* ϯ, the *ch-hei* ϩ.

He reads: ⲃⲓⲕⲭⲓ—Coltsfoot, a sweet, edible plant, growing in clayey soil.

He reads: ⲁϣⲃ—it is a word for which no meaning can be found.

He reads, taking notes, sounding out phrases, compiling growing lists:

ϣⲟⲩⲙⲕ—Streaming eye, a disease—which he is happy to connect with closing of the eye, positing them both as synonyms for blindness

ⲃⲁ—A victor's (martyr's?) crown

ⲥⲙⲟⲡⲧ ⲕⲉⲥⲟⲩ Sⲟⲩⲥⲱⲙⲁ ⲉϥⲟⲩ—A soul passing through closed doors

THE WATCHMEN GET to know him. They see him, hour after hour, as they make their rounds. Even their dogs, Jean François writes his brother, no longer growl.

This, then, is how the young man spends his nights in Paris.

Chapter Nine

On the Soldier's Neck

August, 1798. Cairo.

"I AM YOUR SLAVE," the governor of Alexandria said, surrendering the city to Napoleon. Afterward, he secretly sent a messenger to his Mameluke master in Cairo, describing his desperate bravery in attempting to hold the city and informing him of the approaching danger.

Traveling for days through rough desert terrain, this messenger finally arrives in Cairo at dawn, breathless and exhausted. But just before he enters the city, he is fatally seduced by whirling dervishes dancing by the Nile. Despite having been told to "turn neither to the left nor the right, to salute no man nor to return any man's greetings but to go directly to the Qasr Aini (the Palace of the Fountain)," the messenger dismounts here at the city's edge for the briefest moment—or so he believes—to receive the blessing of the holy men as they spin with flaring robes to beating drums and trilling flutes. Arms outstretched in prayer, their faces are distorted with ecstasy.

Throwing themselves on the ground, they drag him down with them as the Master of the Order gallops over their prostrate bodies on a black stallion, leaving the messenger together with the writhing holy men, who are beyond all care for the vicissitudes of this world.

Thus it is not the messenger who brings the news of the French invasion, but a humble gatherer of *sebak,* of fertilizer, who happens to be passing by. His cart is filled with the crumbled brick of ancient monuments and the effluvia of disintegrating mummies, human heads and torsos, mummified ibises and bulls and apes to be crushed into powder and spread over the depleted fields. This illiterate peasant takes the messenger's dispatches to the Qasr al-Aini. The Mameluke leader, Murad bey, reading the letters with astonishment and rage, rewards the *sebak* gatherer for his trouble with death.

And so it comes about that early in the morning on the twentieth of Muharram, as the Arab historian el-Jabarti records, all of Cairo is thrown into an uproar as word spreads: foreigners have invaded. Alexandria, Damietta, and

Rosetta have already fallen and the army of infidels, like a swarm of locusts, is now heading for the capital.

Crowds begin to roam the city, their shouts filling the air as they attack any foreigners they can find: Greek and Italian merchants mostly, along with a well-known diplomat: the Venetian consul Rosetti, on his way to appear before Murad bey.

By a hair's breadth the consul manages to escape, leaving his servants to fend off the attackers. Galloping through twisting back alleys to the centuries-old dungheaps that rise to a hundred feet outside the city gates, he hides amid the refuse all morning. Finally, necessity triumphing over dignity, he exchanges his clothes for those of a beggar picking through the trash. Thus attired, in a tattered robe thrown over rags, he makes his way to the palace.

Here, at the Qasr al-Aini, the grand divan is assembling. The heavy gates have been thrown open and first Abu Bekir *Pasha,* the Turkish sultan's viceroy, enters; then the learned shayks of the Al-Azhar and their disciples (the historian Jabarti among them). Then, most important of all, the twenty-three Mameluke warlords (or *beys*) arrive one by one. Resplendent in finely wrought armor and mounted on magnificent Arabian horses, their appearance inspires awe. The crowd parts as the warriors ride through the gates, each followed by his trusted henchmen together with hundreds of bodyguards armed to the teeth. For in the violent, treacherous world of Mameluke politics this "news" supposedly from Alexandria—even if it is true, even if invaders have, in fact, arrived—might be nothing more than a ruse, perhaps a pretext for their venerable leader, Murad bey, to gather them together and slaughter them to a man.

Nothing is taken for granted by them—except the unquestioning loyalty of the warrior to his bey, to the warlord who bought him as a child or a youth, choosing him for his strength and his intelligence and his youthful, androgynous beauty. For until they mature, the boys are catamites as well as warriors-in-training, adding another motive for discord among the beys. They become rivals in love as well as power. The beauties among the boys are the cause of deadly clashes—abductions, assassinations—struggles that respect no boundaries, leaving a trail of blood running through mosque and palace alike.

Over this violent brotherhood the Turkish sultan rules—in name, at least. His one demand is money, tribute extorted from the toiling *fellahin* or the rich merchants who are beaten on the soles of their feet or covered with honey and exposed to the sun—one way or another every hidden gold *para* is found.

The pasha, the sultan's viceroy, comes next in the line of command, but he is a mere figurehead. The real power rests with the man who, by force and guile, has come to command the Mamelukes, a role played for the time being by Murad bey. He will lead the warriors into battle against the French. Like the perfume he favors—a pure essence, a distillation of crushed black narcissus and jasmine—Murad bey is a pure essence of the Mameluke way of life.

He began life as a captured slave boy and is given to bragging about the high price, the thousand gold dinars he had cost. At forty-seven, Murad is a survivor of countless struggles and intrigues. He had achieved power quickly in his youth, after which he had then been taken off guard by a sudden coup and had just barely escaped death. Fleeing to the desert with a small band, he eluded capture for years, raiding, plundering, keeping up an incessant pressure. Then the day he fought for finally arrived; he returned from the barren wastes to rule in triumph.

His luxurious gardens were laid out in the desert just beyond the city, their vine-covered paths cooled by splashing fountains and redolent with jasmine and myrtle and myrrh. On pleasure boats on the Nile, he held feasts in the grand style, his Spartan figure quickly running to fat. With a library extensive even by Mameluke standards, whose libraries are second in magnificence only to their tombs, Murad is read to by a troop of sweet-voiced boys, since he himself cannot read.

Wily and boastful, known to be cruelest when he

appears most mild, most dangerous when his voice becomes soft and caressing, like water running over pebbles, the fleshy Murad bey presents a complete contrast to the one rival he has not been able to subdue and with whom he has formed an uneasy partnership: the dour, ascetic Ibrahim bey. Older than Murad by some twenty years, Ibrahim is as silent as Murad is expansive, as stingy as his counterpart is extravagant. Punctilious about fast days and prayers, he is a man whom it is deadly to cross, having cast his net—an army of spies and assassins—over the land.

On important occasions, such as the grand divan that has now assembled, Murad defers to his partner in public, elaborately showing Ibrahim respect and courtesy. In fact, Murad is the one with the greater power and the one who has the final say. Still, with a dissimulation second nature in the Mameluke world, Murad allows his rival pride of place: Ibrahim is the one who speaks first and who calls himself by the loftier title, *Shayk el Balad,* Ruler of the Land, while Murad is merely *Emir el Haj,* Ruler of the Pilgrimage.

Tall and thin, hollow-cheeked from fasting, Ibrahim speaks briefly and in a voice which barely rises above a whisper. Until one of his bodyguards repeats his words, they can not be heard in the great hall. And when they *are* heard—"The walls of Cairo are high and thick. Let us await the French behind them"—pandemonium breaks loose. The beys reject such caution with scorn and laughter.

Accusations follow: the pasha is charged with having connived with the foreigners for his own reasons. After all, could the French have landed in Egypt without the Turkish sultan's knowledge? The pasha denies such complicity, blaming the beys for the poor showing at Alexandria. Nothing less than treason, he claims. Recriminations fly thick and fast, it is all the historian Jabarti can do to record a part of them. One after the other, each of the beys and shayks has his say.

". . . until finally, the shayk [Mukru'um Sa'ad] arose and cried: 'All this is a result of negligence in managing the ports and lettings things come to such a pass that the enemy could occupy it.'

"Hearing which, Murad bey exclaimed: 'What can we do? For whenever I want to rebuild and fortify you claim: *Their intention* [at Alexandria and Rosetta] *is rebellion.* And this is what has prevented me from acting.'

"Such were his excuses," Jabarti sighs, "as frail as a spider's web, for since the time of Ali bey, not only did he not pay sufficient attention to the ports but even removed what weapons and cannons were already there! Furthermore, he stopped the flow of ammunition, and furthermore . . ." etc., etc. Murad, distrustful of his own people, has left them unprepared for an attack.

Spies arrive to report on what they have seen: The French cavalry is practically nonexistent, they say. The invaders are struggling to cross the desert *on foot*—news which leads to more scorn and laughter. Is it not obvious that foot soldiers have no chance against the Mameluke cavalry? The foreigners are doomed, that is clear to see, and the argument becomes who will have the honor of being first to ride out and "greet" them.

And in the midst of the tumult and debate, a single voice is raised in agreement with Ibrahim's caution, the voice of a hated foreigner who has spent the morning hiding in a dungheap! While the Venetian consul has, of course, washed and changed, word of his indignity makes the beys greet him with derision. But when the consul begins to describe this Bonaparte as a dangerous warrior, an invincible leader who has already proved his valor, laughter changes to sullen silence. Finally his words go beyond what Murad can bear. He cuts him short with curses and boasts echoed by those of the other beys who make the palace resound with their shouts.

The debate proceeds, shouts slowly dying into discrete and whispered conversations until finally, bit by bit, they piece together a plan of action. Despite their mutual distrust and internecine quarrels, they in advance divvy up the loot and the glory and the slaves which will soon be theirs.

It is late by the time that they have settled the fate of the French to their satisfaction. The capture of "Bunbarte," the general, Murad bey claims for his own. Having finished their work, the divan is adjourned and the solemn procession rides forth from the palace: the pasha, the learned shayks, and the tall, swaggering, luxury-loving, tomb-designing, book-collecting beys together with their bodyguards, armed to the teeth, and their beautiful pages, blue-eyed and blond and fair—boys with much the same looks their masters had when kidnapped from the Caucasus a decade or two before.

The gold and silver of their armor shine in the bonfires lit at the palace gates. And then they are gone and the fires are extinguished, leaving behind a reflective witness. The historian Jabarti notes everything, remembers everything, and is filled with foreboding as "the raven of darkness spread its black wings over the Palace of the Fountain . . ."

And over Cairo . . . and over the path that lay ahead.

П口口

FOR MANY OF the Frenchmen crossing the desert, Jabarti's "raven" descends suddenly and during the day. The darkness begins as a sensation: a burning under the eyelids.

After which, the fierce glare of the sun becomes dimmer. The soldier experiences the blessed relief of shade as he marches through the barren land. The blindness that follows means certain death for him at this stage of the campaign. He is alone in the vast desert, his comrades have no way of helping him.

It is all they can do to keep going themselves. Marching over rocks and sand in temperatures in the 120s, their small allotment of water is used up right away by men too thirsty to restrain themselves. Many perish within the first hours of the forced march, struck down by the blistering heat and exhaustion. An officer, Belliard, will recall: ". . . a melancholy settled over us as we came to Birket [a mere twenty miles from Alexandria] for the numbers of those dying from thirst increased . . . soldiers tumbling onto the sand dunes never to rise again."

With terrible suffering, the French crawl over the short space of earth separating Alexandria from Birket, a town which, it turns out, is nothing more than a name given to sand and rocks surrounding a dry canal. If the seasonal flood of the Nile had been higher, the troops would have found some respite.

But the Nile is low and the men are forced to march on, many soldiers leaving their provisions and ammunition behind in a desperate attempt to lighten their burdens. After all, even if they were able to eat it, hard, dry biscuit would only increase their thirst. And why should men too weary to hold a gun continue to carry loads of ammunition?

"The scorching air parched our throats," another officer remembers, "and it was with difficulty that we moved our arms or legs or even drew breath . . ."

Yet, as the men begin their first night in the desert, General Desaix begins to speak to the disheartened men as Napoleon would: of glory. Like Napoleon, Desaix had his beginnings in the revolutionary army as a young, talented soldier with nothing to support him but his enthusiasm. From the first, he had recognized Napoleon's superiority, recording early on in his diary, "I am persuaded that Bonaparte will achieve so immense a glory that it will reflect on his lieutenants . . . He is proud, hidden, never forgives. And he vows to follow his enemy to the end of the world."

Now, however, Desaix is beginning to see at just what price this glory will be won. Though he tries to rouse his men with Napoleonic phrases, he is no Napoleon. He suffers with his men, reserving for himself scarcely more than they have, but he cannot make them forget their sufferings as Napoleon would have, as much with his demonic energy as by his words. Desaix cannot fill them with resolve or bring them to ecstasy with a piercing look filled with "fate."

Napoleon is preoccupied with more mundane matters just now. If he is a demon, he is a practical one and realizes that he must leave behind a well-organized occupation at

Alexandria before moving on to Cairo. When he does join the troops in a day or two, unlike Desaix, he will cross the desert quickly, on horseback and with a plentiful supply of water and wine, and a tent to retire to when the sun is at its height. Like a being from another world, he will insist on a full military review, all spit and polish, and then swoop down on the men with threats and honors, awarding medals to the brave like the emperor he will soon be—and vowing to shoot all cowards and defeatists.

If he cannot inspire the men, Desaix can, at least, give them *hope*—"that bedraggled daughter of fear and desire." In another day, they will be at El Beydah, with its cisterns and its date palms and sheep, and they can begin to live off the land as they had done during the conquest of Italy.

Speeches done, Desaix turns into an army chaplain or father confessor, reading to the exhausted soldiers from Montesquieu—whose works, together with those of Voltaire and Rousseau, must take the place of prayer for the excommunicated Frenchmen.

And so it is to the *rational* lullaby of Montesquieu's *Spirit of the Laws*—as opposed to the old "Roman absurdities"— that the soldiers fall into a fitful sleep under the desert sky: "Laws, taken in the broadest meaning, are the necessary relations deriving from the nature of things; and in this sense, all beings have their laws. . . . the material world. . . . the beasts of the fields have their laws, man has his laws.

Those who have said . . ." On and on, as the wind blows the sand over the exhausted men until reveille sounds at 2 AM. It seems to them that they have just closed their eyes and they begin to march again.

Hauling themselves and their baggage carts and whatever artillery they have managed to load onto limbers and caissons through the soft sand into which they sink up to their ankles, they try to cover as much territory as they can while it is still night. For with the sunrise, the torture begins anew.

Soldiers chase mirages, pools of blue water which appear on the horizon. The Frenchmen fling themselves into imaginary water which turns to sand again and again until, tortured by the illusion, some shoot themselves in despair.

Their feet are blistered from the fine sand which they cannot keep out of their boots. Their uniforms are absurdly heavy. Driven mad by the heat, men rip off their jackets and even their shirts, exposing fair skin to the desert sun. They leave behind a trail of splendid military attire, powder blue or dark green with gold facings, and stiff army caps with plumes of red and white . . . all borne to oblivion by the desert wind.

Hour after hour: surrounded by the everlasting sameness of the desert, the heat, the silence, the glare of the sun, the men collapsing, the monotonous rhythm of the march. The monotony is broken when it is least expected by the shock of attack. Bedouins suddenly appear from behind the dunes, shooting as they ride at full gallop, hurling javelins or thrusting their swords at the unwary, then disappearing again into the desert.

Ten, sometimes twenty fall during such raids, regretted less than the wounding or capture of the few precious animals. It is the horses and donkeys who help drag the weapons Napoleon has decided will be key to victory: the big guns, howitzers, and cannons.

To keep knowledge of them from the enemy until the very last minute, they are covered with canvas and surrounded by an elite guard as they approach El Beydah, where, Desaix fears, Murad bey might have stationed spies.

The precaution is unnecessary: El Beydah is desolate. Not a soul stirs within its mud-brick houses. Its few palms have been stripped of dates and even of branches. The two cisterns have been filled with rocks and sand.

"If the whole army does not cross the desert with the speed of lightning, it will perish . . ." Desaix writes to Napoleon, begging for medicine and provisions, sacrificing one of his precious horses for the messenger. "Our guides have misled us and fled. Do not leave us in this situation for the troops are beginning to give up."

Meanwhile, a desperate fight breaks out around the cisterns which have been quickly cleared. From them a rivulet of muddy water flows. Those who throw themselves on the ground to drink are trampled to death by thousands struggling to get to the water. And though guns are used to restore order, before long the whole business becomes futile—the cisterns are drained dry. When he tries to calm them with promises, which even he does not believe, that food and water are just a day's march away, Desaix is almost stoned by the angry men.

囗 囗 囗

DAMANHUR, *RIVER OF BLOOD,* a place named for the deep red its cliffs and dunes turn in the light of the setting sun.

Here Desaix and his troops are joined by a second, and then a third division from Cairo; and then by Napoleon himself. So far he has ignored the appeals of Desaix and the other generals, waiting until now to give them his answer. They want water, medicine, provisions? They will get everything they want when they reach Cairo.

The troops need victory, Napoleon tells them during a war conference held in an old barn. That will put an end to all this whining. And a victory is just what he proposes to give them, he adds.

After this rousing speech, General Mireur rides into the desert and shoots himself, unable to endure any more suffering. His men search for him and, by nightfall, they find him, vultures leading them to his beribboned and bemedaled body. He had even donned his tricolor sash of honor before killing himself. As the sun sets and the desert turns its deep, deep red, they bury him near the cliffs at the edge of the town, medals, sash, and all. The carrion birds continue circling overhead.

It is a fitting burial place. The cliffs that look down upon the grave are covered with graffiti: curses scratched onto the rocks by other solders who have also passed this way. Greeks and Romans crossed the desert in the days when Damanhur was Hermopolis Parva, city of Hermes to the Greeks (Thoth to the Egyptians). A god thrice blessed and thrice great, Hermes Trismegistos, created a deep mystery—the *neter tched,* the words of the gods, breath—fleeting sound made immortal through writing.

If the exhausted French soldiers digging Mireur's grave had not been so busy with their task, if they had had enough strength, food, and water to permit them to think of something besides drawing their next breath, they might have lingered before these scribblings on the cliffs—these epitaphs for Mireur and all their other comrades who have fallen so far.

For while the drawings etched onto the rocks are light-hearted enough—for example, a hunchbacked, pot-bellied dwarf plays on a flute; and a bald-headed old priest, censer in hand, sports with two naked girls—while the doodlings here are whimsical or even obscene, the writing, carved in Greek and Latin, sounds a different note.

Scratched on the stone along with the many names of Greek mercenaries and Roman legionnaires on one expedition or another, the writing tells of soldiers on their way to quell a rebellion or to collect taxes, or to take prisoners to the mines and the quarries in the south.

Like the French these ancient soldiers are footsore and hungry and curse the heat and the sand and the scorpions and vipers hidden under every rock. Longing for home, they precede the grumbling of Napoleon's men with their emphatic "Shit!" or "To hell with this land!"—their unhappiness echoing across the long perspective of time.

Far beneath the cliffs, deep under the sand, rolled up in pottery jars or hidden in the coffins of the mummified ibises and baboons (animals sacred to Thoth), are papyri which record the miseries of other soldiers, Egyptians who preceded the Greeks—who preceded the Romans—who preceded the French. In their time, these warriors had also hungered and thirsted and waded, as the French do now, through the "river of blood":

He is awakened after only an hour and they prod him
like a donkey.
He is hungry, his belly aching.
He is dead while alive.

He is ordered far away, to Syria or Cush.
He gets neither food nor sandals when they give out the supplies.
He marches while the sun is hot and burning overhead.

Only on the third day can he drink foul water that tastes like salt.
Diarrhea tears his stomach.
The enemies come and he is surrounded in combat.

Arrows take his life from him
As his leader shouts:
"Attack brave warrior! Get a name for yourself!"

But he does not know what has happened to his body.
His aching legs give way.
If victory comes, the plunder and slaves must be carried back to
Pharaoh in Egypt.

The foreign slave woman can walk no further.
She is put on the soldier's neck.
His own wife and children wait for him in their town.
But he has fallen

He is dead.
He never reaches home.

They leave behind their record as the French soldiers will leave behind theirs: memoirs and histories and even their names, Jacques or Jean or Lieutenant so-and-so of the 5th Chasseurs, scratched on rocks and temple walls.

Ancient words come down through the centuries in Egyptian and Greek, in Latin and French—half lament, half boast uttered with a melancholy smile.

Words with no other moral than to say: Look at us! Like you, we are human beings— —*tears of the gods.* Comrades in arms: of the Regiment of Seth: Senbi. Senwosret of the Regiment of Ra. Meryptah, who carries the king's placenta when we go forth into battle.

These are our names and the honors we hold. Do not forget us till **hhehh,** —the end of time.

□ □ □

AT A PLACE called Rahmaniya, *the Merciful,* the belea-
guered Frenchmen finally arrive at the Nile. There is water
and shade here. There are the promised palm trees heavy
with clusters of ripe dates, and lemon and orange and fig
trees as well, and black currants, and watermelons, fields
and fields of them.

Some men begin by gorging themselves on the fruit.
Others strip off their uniforms or leap into the river fully
clothed, shouting for joy.

On this day of rejoicing, the feast of St. Watermelon, the
men laughingly call it, Murad bey and his Mamelukes suddenly appear. Armed with helmets, spears, sabers, lances,
axes, daggers, and pistols, mounted on beautiful Arabian
horses, they look down from the hills east of the Nile.

The naked men in the water, stunned, fall silent.

Chapter Ten

Of Linguists and Emperors
and Everlasting Fame

1823. Italy.

ON A HOT day in the middle of August, a swarthy man with dark eyes pores over an ancient scroll. The room is small and airless, a stone chamber in an Italian palazzo where many miscellaneous finds have been carelessly stored. Although the man is just in his thirties, his hands tremble perpetually and he is stooped as he reads. At that moment he, Jean François Champollion, is the only person in the world who can understand the ancient writing on the coffins and statues surrounding him, or so he thinks. *Could it be? Does he know the truth or not? Are his enemies right to mock him?*

Champollion has claimed that this is a system of writing and he understands the seemingly endless number of beautiful and bizarre and sometimes grotesque pictures. There are thousands of them. Has he deluded himself? Is he mad? He insists that he has deciphered Egyptian writing. He has staked his reputation on his claim—but is it true that the disembodied hands and legs, the stars and scepters and staring eyes form words, that they speak to him and to him alone after a silence of fifteen hundred years?

Ignoring his exhaustion, Champollion persists in his patient, obscure work. Throughout his life, the rhythm of his existence is twofold: periods of almost monastic withdrawal from the world and intense lonely toil, alternate with periods of great excitement and public debate. But always the burden of the past weighs heavily. There is the crushing, painstaking labor which proceeds picture by picture, sign by sign, word by word.

Time falls away as Champollion slowly reads this ancient document, teasing out its meaning. It is a tale of passion and betrayal, a story of two thousand years before . . . in Egypt . . . as the Nile rises for its yearly flooding, bringing its rich, dark silt to the parched land.

People rejoice, breaking off from their labors, and in the midst of the celebrations, a beautiful woman leaves her husband to run away with her lover.

The woman's name is not recorded. Or perhaps it is

written on part of the scroll which has crumbled to dust in this small, stifling chamber of the palazzo. So, while she is nameless, the record states that she is tall and beautiful and dark, from the southern reaches of the divided kingdom, perhaps a Nubian. Running away with one of the foreign soldiers who have occupied northern Egypt, she abandons her two young daughters. About their Egyptian father, the story is silent. These forlorn girls are taken in by a relative to live in the city dedicated to the crocodile-headed god, Sobek.

Raised in the temple of Sobek, the two girls serve the living incarnation of the god: a huge crocodile who lazes in the sun, a glittering beast with jewels and gold sewn into its hide. One of the girls, no older than fourteen, becomes a temple prostitute, selling her body in honor of the monstrous deity. She splits her earnings with the bald-headed priests who in turn divide their share: a part for themselves, a part for the reptile-god whom they anoint with oils and perfumed unguents after offering him choice meat and game.

A year goes by and again, during the Inundation, the mother reappears. She talks her prostitute-daughter into giving up her savings: her mother promises to find her a husband. The money will be used both for the dowry and for the cliterectomy, the female castration that will make her child a better match. But the wayward mother is false in her promises and, instead of finding a husband for her daughter, she runs away with her daughter's savings.

A temple hermit recounts the details in brilliantly colored hieroglyphs. About him we know only that he has retired to the precincts of the sacred pool where the god lives. Night after night he gazes on the bejeweled beast, praying to be granted prophetic dreams, visions which would catapult him to fame and honor at the pharaoh's court. At the young girl's request, he writes her tale of woe as a legal complaint.

Whether the authorities act on it, what happens to the girl, her mother, her sister, the temple recluse, we do not know. The scroll on which the story was written is kept with other such documents which remained in the great archives of the temple for hundreds of years. And then, finally, during the fourth century AD, the hieroglyphic script in which these documents are written goes out of use. The meaning of the strange symbols is forgotten. And for fifteen hundred years they remain a mystery, along with all the other inscriptions and carvings and paintings from this ancient world.

⊓ ⊓ ⊓

A CARETAKER KNOCKS on the door but is sent away. Since coming to Turin, Champollion has been so forgetful of his appearance and surroundings that the servants have begun to whisper that he is not quite right. The scroll before him has not yielded its meaning easily: The complex writing presents endless difficulties, endless exceptions to principles he himself had discovered earlier, when he had made his great breakthrough.

He had been going along in the path which had been trod by scholars struggling with the hieroglyphs since the Renaissance, when suddenly he understood: first one word, then two, then the principle, the key which unlocked the mystery.

Half-mad then with excitement he had run through the streets of Paris to the library where his brother worked. Holding his tattered notebook out to the astonished Jacques, he shouted, *"Je tiens l'affair!* (I've done it!)" Then he fainted, falling into a coma and lying unconscious for eight days, more dead than alive.

From the first announcement of his discovery, it is fiercely disputed; the British especially cover him with scorn and fiercely contest his findings. Champollion's theories are contrary to the ideas held about hieroglyphics from the earliest time, ideas which he himself had espoused until, in a moment of inspiration, all his years of study, all the concentrated effort of a lifetime, bore fruit.

The challenge now is proving what he knows. The first basis for Champollion's conclusions had been the Rosetta stone, but this monument was not enough to refute his critics. True, the stone was inscribed both in hieroglyphic and Greek and by comparing the scripts, one could arrive at certain possibilities. But the inferences drawn from the stone are still only educated guesses, mere clues and theories.

First, the Greek and Egyptian writing on the stone are paraphrases of each other. They give the general meaning of the decree, and are not word-for-word translations. Also, the writing on the stone is dismissed by the experts as providing too small a sample to conclusively prove any theory. It contains only fourteen lines of formal hieroglyphs: a slender basis for Champollion's claim that he can read the hieroglyphs.

The brilliant Englishman Thomas Young, physicist, physician, amateur classicist, had briefly studied the stone. He made a limited but important contribution to its decipherment before giving up. A wealthy and sophisticated scholar with a broad range of interests, Young makes Champollion, with his lifelong devotion to this one mystery, seem like a crank. Champollion, holed up in a cheap rooming house in Paris, lives for one reason and for one reason alone: the hieroglyphs.

From this obscurity, Champollion announces to the world that he can read them. Young, writing at ease from a fashionable seaside resort, gives his verdict: "Champollion is wrong."

The burden of proof falls on Champollion. But in the time which has passed since his great discovery, physical ailments ravage the obsessed scholar. Intense intellectual effort and the struggle with poverty have taken their toll on the slender, handsome young man, prematurely aging him.

The race to confirm his discoveries is also a race with death, whose presence Champollion is not allowed to forget as he studies funerary papyri, coffin texts, and ancient dirges.

The question is, will Champollion's discoveries be his "calling card on Immortality," as he has put it in a letter to his brother, or will his work be dismissed as the egotistical ravings of a madman?

London. A darkened room where a single, narrow beam of light falls on a human eye.

The light illuminates this and nothing more. It is a patient's eye, its pupil dilating and contracting as the doctor, Thomas Young, observes intently. This is how his waking hours are largely spent, observing and analyzing and collecting data as he sees patients and conducts experiments. You can see in his pale, thoughtful, otherworldly, abstracted face that he is a man who has had more nights than days in his life.

The light itself becomes the object of his study: candlelight shining through (or made "coherent" by) funnel-like shades and colored filters of blue and green and violet and red. In his most famous experiment, Dr. Young demonstrates the undulatory or wave theory of light which overturns Newton's particle theory. But still, despite his considerable achievement, Young is dissatisfied and restless, plagued by what Milton calls "that last failing of a noble mind": the thirst for fame.

He pursues other investigations—the nature of color; and astigmatism; and the manner in which the eye accommodates itself to distance. But in the wake of Napoleon's campaign, as volume after volume of *The Description of Egypt* is published and thousands of scrolls and antiquities find their way to Europe, it is not talk of the nature of astigmatism or of color or light which is on everyone's lips, but the meaning of the hieroglyphs. Though no linguist, Young now takes up the problem. He brings to his study a thorough classical education and finely honed analytic skills, as well as the pride of a (so far) undefeated intellect.

While Young pursues his intellectual quarry at his ease, a letter arrives from the village of Figeac. A schoolmaster there working with illiterate peasant children requests that the secretary of the Royal Society (Young) furnish him with clarification of some details about the stone which are obscure on his copy. Young, none too pleased to be hearing from a rival, replies that the obscurities on the copy are also unclear on the original.

The provincial schoolmaster is none other than Jean François, who is languishing in "internal exile," a richly deserved punishment. For Jean François had taken up Napoleon's cause just as Napoleon was going down to defeat.

Jean François had been opposed to the emperor during the years of the glorious French victories. The linguist had all along opposed the tyranny of the high-handed Bonaparte. But now, in Napoleon's final days, the empire doomed and dying, the Bourbons waiting in the wings about to return, Jean François—idealist, romantic, fool—publicly plants the tricolor on the walls of Grenoble's fort during the allied siege.

For if Napoleon is a tyrant, if the emperor is high-handed and authoritarian, at least his tyranny is more bearable than that of the reactionary Bourbons. At least it is in the name of an ideal. The Bourbons represent the mindless return to the stultifying past. Of the Bourbons, the dreary Louis XVIII and, even worse, his arrogant brother Charles X, it is truly said that they had forgotten nothing (of their privileges) and had learned nothing (during their long exile).

Thus Champollion becomes a "Bonapartist" just in time to be branded as persona non grata by the returning Bourbons, ensuring that both he and, by association, his brother will suffer.

Jean François has not that much to lose, for up until now his professional life has consisted of meager appointments: assistant professor (at half salary, given his youth) or sub-librarian or unpaid assistant to his brother in Paris or Grenoble. They are appointments which are given and then taken away as the political situation fluctuates. During difficult periods, his brother supports him for months at a time.

He undergoes the desperation of being down and out and knowing—trying not to lose sight of the knowledge—that if only he can continue on his path, his name will echo throughout eternity. It is the kind of struggle to which Dostoyevsky refers when he speculates that Columbus was happiest ten minutes *before* he discovered America—though perhaps without knowing it himself . . . when his sailors cursed him and mutinied; when he was straining against overwhelming obstacles; when success or failure still hung in the balance; when he was filled with self-doubt and misgivings.

If this struggle is what constitutes true happiness—if victory is merely a somnolent, posthumous, half-and-half state—then perhaps for Jean François this might be called a time of true joy.

Proud; solitary among the crowds of Paris; his clothes in tatters so that, he writes his brother in Grenoble, he is ashamed to go out in decent society. He resents being sent on endless errands for his brother, who chastises him as if he were a young boy. Defiant, knowing his own worth, he is nevertheless humbled by having to take charity from a brother with little enough for himself and his family. He translates, not the Rosetta stone, but some sensational Italian novel for a small fee so that he can get by.

Once the restoration of the Bourbons takes place, he is no longer even the occasional "assistant to an assistant," the underpaid professor, or librarian's secretary.

For a time, he works with poor children, trying to introduce the Lancaster system, a new method of education which advocates not only teaching children how to read but teaching them how to teach other children to read as well— the older teaching the younger. Behind the idea is the hope that learning will thus spread throughout the countryside like ripples in a pool: a goal strongly opposed by the church and the political conservatives who see universal literacy as a threat to the returning stability of the old order. Thus this activity makes Jean François even more suspect.

And as if the burden of supporting himself is not enough,

he has taken on the responsibility of a wife along the way. A girl of sixteen whom he had met in Grenoble, defies her bourgeois father for his sake. It is not only her father who opposes the marriage, but Jean François' brother is against the match as well. Appalled by the girl's ignorance, Jacques refuses to attend the wedding, predicting misery for both.

The two lovers are engaged for years. By the time they finally marry, Jean François' interest in her has waned and he marries her out of a sense of duty and gratitude. As he later writes in a letter, it would have been dishonorable to break off the engagement after Rosine's long faithfulness to him, her defiance of her family, her steadfast rejection of more eligible suitors, etc.

It is hard to say how true this picture of their marriage is, and how much of it is a retrospective view colored by the fact that at the time he writes the letter not only he is looking back over the distance of some years, but he is alone. He has left Rosine behind to continue his researches in Italy. And what's more, the letter is addressed to a brilliant young woman he meets here, Angelica Palli.

She is everything his wife is not. For while the interests of Champollion's wife do not extend beyond family and home, Angelica is accomplished, intellectual, and fascinated by his work.

She is also unattainable. Married to an Italian nobleman with whom she will live in aristocratic ease, she bequeaths to posterity thirty passionate letters, the feeling in them all the more palpable for what is left unsaid.

These letters are not written in Coptic or Arabic or Latin or Greek, but in the language—where can he have learned it, poring over old, musty papyri night and day as he does?—the language of love.

॰॰॰

"THE RING" . . . painted on countless papyri, engraved on statues, chiseled on the walls of tombs and the sides of obelisks, an oval ring winds around a cluster of hieroglyphs, thus—

Setting off certain hieroglyphs from the rest, the ring is the first clue in the decipherment. It is guessed that these rings enclose the names of the foreign as well as the native pharoahs, and that therefore these foreign names must somehow have been written phonetically. That is, the sounds of these names would need to come into play as there would be no way to represent foreign names with symbols alone. The guess uses Chinese as an analogy, Chinese being another language that is written with symbols derived from pictures; another language in which *sound* and *writing* part ways, and another language which encloses foreign names in a ring.

The savants who accompany Bonaparte's army to Egypt call the rings "cartouches"—cartridges—after the oval shaped ammunition of the soldiers' guns.

This first clue, this French "cartridge" enclosing Egyptian writing, is a fitting metaphor for linguist and emperor, for thought entangled in the world, for the power which encircles knowledge and the violence which claims it for its own.

ロ ロ ロ

"THE BOOK"—Horapollo's *Hieroglyphica*—another early clue, is discovered in the 1400s on Andros, a Greek island in the Mediterranean, by a shepherd wandering in the mountains.

Noticing the entrance to a cave, an opening so narrow that it might be nothing more than a crevice in the steep face of the cliff, he had climbed up to explore, crawling into the darkness where at first he finds nothing.

Nothing worth risking his neck for, that is: amphorae, ancient wine jars of the kind once used in libations, and only fragments of them at that, broken shards heaped in a pile. But under the jars, miraculously preserved, is an ancient book—more than a thousand years old, it will be ascertained—which the shepherd takes away as a prize.

Written in Egyptian in the fourth century AD by Horapollo and translated into Greek by a certain "Philip"— so the book states—it is the only surviving ancient work which has as its subject the meaning of the hieroglyphs. Of the book's author, Horapollo (Horus + Apollo), nothing is known except that, given his name, he must have been a hellenized Egyptian. It can also be conjectured that he had decided to record whatever he knew about the hieroglyphs before they were supplanted by the Greek alphabet and forgotten.

"A baboon can stand for either the moon or the world," the author declares, "or writing or anger. A donkey's head is used for a man who has never traveled and knows nothing of the world. And a hand is used for a builder, since the hand performs the work," etc., etc. The book provides a word list or a sign list, a dictionary of key symbols, king, priest, the Nile. More important, its translations reveal the principle, the method by which the hieroglyphics are to be read. It is a system in which the pictures become symbols sometimes taking on one, sometimes many meanings.

And so the rare book is an important find, acquiring great authority during the Renaissance. It passes hands many times—from shepherd to merchant to prince—finally arriving in Rome, where the pope, Sixtus IV, is in the midst of gathering countless rare manuscripts. Buying them up on a grand scale, he adds them to his predecessor's modest collection and houses them in style, creating one of the great libraries of the world.

Throughout the 1470s, book dealers of every description are sure to find a welcome in the Vatican, as are spies and desperados. For Sixtus is in the midst of a life-and-death struggle with the Medicis of Florence.

Sixtus wants the Medici brothers out of the way. And he wants Horapollo's *Hieroglyphica* . . . and Plutarch's *Isis and Osiris* and whatever fragments of Manetho's *Chronology of the Pharaohs* can be found scattered among the ancient manuscripts—and Polybius' *Histories* with their long parentheses on the Ptolemies of Egypt . . . and an extensive list of Coptic works, works which centuries later Jean François will study in Paris.

But the principles Horapollo explains, and even most of the meanings he gives for the hieroglyphs, are not correct.

Though the book contains grains of truth, these grains are mixed with mountains of imagination at such an unequal proportion as to make them useless to a linguist. And these false clues lead generations of scholars astray, from the fifteenth century of Sixtus' Rome right until the nineteenth century when Champollion studies Horapollo's writing and absorbs his many errors.

SIXTUS' GREAT LIBRARY comes to be built in the midst of bloodshed and intrigue. The Medicis are attacked in church on Easter Sunday: Taken unawares, one brother is killed while the other manages to escape, leading to war between Florence and Rome. And if it is a wonder that Sixtus, though so embattled, occupies himself with his books and his library, it is a wonder that Napoleon repeats four centuries later, also while in the midst of the sharpest crisis of his life. Escaping from Elba in the spring of 1815, Napoleon arrives in the south of France and makes a desperate bid to regain his lost empire.

The fugitive emperor is met by a crowd of fervent worshippers, loyal old soldiers and young boys thirsting for glory. Their number swells to a thousand as Napoleon heads north toward Grenoble where the Fifth Regiment is stationed: more than seven thousand men and heavy cannon. The regimental commander, sworn to protect the restored Bourbons, dispatches a detachment of well-armed soldiers to capture Bonaparte, sending a message to Paris that he has the situation well in hand. He assumes it will be a simple matter to subdue the rebels. Indeed, his men have no trouble finding Napoleon: Just south of the city, they come upon the ragtag crowd following the ex-Emperor.

Before any fighting can take place, though, Napoleon strides out to face his pursuers. Throwing open his military coat, he declares: "You seek your emperor. I am here! Kill me if you wish!"

In silence, the amazed soldiers face the living embodiment of French glory. Suddenly, the defeats and hardships of the past are forgotten. The Bourbons mean nothing. The soldiers cannot repudiate Napoleon. Amid cheers and shouts of "Long live the Emperor!" the men are suddenly Napoleon's once again. They accompany him to the city, which receives him with a joyous celebration that continues throughout the night.

Establishing temporary headquarters in the mayor's office, Napoleon sends countless orders and proclamations and letters to every part of France, commanding, imploring old comrades-in-arms to stand by him now. In the midst of all his feverish activity, a delegation of professors from the university arrives.

Champollion is among them. The occasion calls for a few formal phrases, the scholars have only come to pay their respects. But as the delegation withdraws, Napoleon is struck by Champollion's appearance and manner and he questions him about his work. The young linguist's opinions interest him. Does Jean François think the decipherment of the Rosetta stone a real possibility? Does he think ancient Egyptian has a complicated grammar, declensions, a subjunctive? The subjunctive! With the future of not only France but all Europe at stake, the two men talk of Egyptian grammar which Champollion conjectures would resemble that of Coptic.

Coptic, the pharaohs, the savants' engravings of the monuments, Denon's sketches: The two men sit talking late into the night.

Napoleon knows much about Egypt, not only as a general but as a student, having attended many sessions of the institute he founded in Cairo. When the ferocious heat of the day relented at twilight, it was Napoleon's habit to appear in the garden of the exquisite palace reserved for the scholars' use. Toasts were proposed, a good excuse for the wine to flow, as discoveries were announced: the exact measurements of the sphinx, a new species of bird found in the marshes, a temple half sunk in the sand, a successful treatment for the eye disease so prevalent in Egypt.

If Champollion contradicts the emperor on some points, Napoleon allows it. There is no question of lèse-majesté. Both see the world from an eagle's vantage point, ranging over continents and millennia to draw their conclusions.

Napoleon promises to rush Champollion's huge work on Coptic through the imperial press, a promise undone one hundred days later by Waterloo. The combined British, Prussian, Austrian, and Russian forces defeat Napoleon, and the British government sends him to his final exile on St. Helena. Jean Francois' definitive Coptic dictionary will never see the light of day.

But even on St. Helena—on this small, remote island in the South Atlantic, a scrap of black volcanic rock surrounded by endless ocean—Napoleon clings to the "ideal."

Jagged cliffs rise from the ocean on all sides. Perched high on one of the cliffs is a country house in which the prisoner-emperor lies dying. His body puffy with disease, his features sunk in fat, and his eyes surrounded by dark shadows, he talks of a hundred possible projects as if he were still the new Prometheus. He rants about land recla-mation—like Goethe's Faust in the second part of the epic poem, another hero in a sequel who spends his days using science to reclaim land, handful by handful, from the sea.

Power or knowledge, knowledge or power. When all is said and done, which is the shadow and which is the substance? Which is worth having? Which is worth striving for?

Chapter Eleven

The Weight of the World

August 1922. Cairo. The Abdin Palace.

SIGNOR GIOVANNI MARRA, a historian dressed in a formal morning suit, and suffering in the intense heat, nervously waits in the enormous reception room for the arrival of the king, Fuad.

The palace is meant to be grand, with high ceilings and marble floors and much gilt and carved wood. There is something depressing about the official rooms. An imitation of a Western notion of what is royal, they are like a stage setting where Fuad can play at being king for the benefit of the foreign diplomats and visiting dignitaries.

Small signs of shabbiness everywhere surprise and even scandalize the rather stupid Signor Marra. Like a housekeeper, he meticulously notes the defects in his memoirs: the silk wallpaper is stained here and there by swatted insects; the drapes are frayed though they hang from magnificently gilded cornices; the vitrines containing medals and ribbons and coins are dusty and even cracked, etc.

It is as if Fuad, demoralized by the presence of the British, has let things go—an inference Signor Marra does not draw. Indeed, he is the kind of historian who comes to few conclusions, being content merely to record what he can.

A servant in livery interrupts these observations to lead him to the king, who is walking in the garden. The royal greets his visitor in a high-pitched drawl, interrupted every few words with a harsh, guttural bark. A bullet is lodged in Fuad's throat, fired by a half-mad cousin. Visitors are warned to take no notice of the noises which punctuate His Majesty's conversation.

The interview succeeds in winning Signor Marra the permission he needs. He is the first foreigner to be given access to the lower vaults of the Citadel, Saladin's sprawling twelfth-century fortress which dominates the city.

In the dark, airless chambers, amid snakes and rats, Marra finds the moldering records he has been seeking, accounts which go back to the short period when Napoleon ruled—or rather, *tried* to rule—Cairo. Calling himself "Sultan Kebir," the Great Sultan, Napoleon issues endless edicts and dispenses "enlightened" humane justice—justice which becomes less enlightened and more harsh and even barbaric as Napoleon learns the bitter lesson that to capture a great foreign city is not the same as to hold it.

⊓ ⊓ ⊓

1798. SHUBRA KIT. A place near the watermelon patches of Rahmaniya and the Nile. In the annals of military history, the first encounter between Napoleon's troops and the Mamelukes—an insignificant skirmish at a place named Shubra Kit—is passed over in silence.

Instead, when the battles of the First Empire come to be taught in the military academies of France's Second Empire, attention is focused on the great struggle that takes place on the vast plain before Cairo, with its larger-than-life proportions and its ancient pyramids looming in the background.

Yet it is during this first skirmish that the basic approaches of the adversaries are put to the test. Napoleon puts his faith in strategy and calculation here. Whatever heavy artillery he has managed to drag over the desert he now uses with mathematical precision. The Mameluke leader, Murad, relies on the desperate personal courage of his men, and on his vastly superior cavalry.

There are the infinite number of incalculable elements involved in any battle. Napoleon's men are exhausted, demoralized, and on the point of open rebellion. After the brutal desert crossing, when Napoleon had first reappeared among them, he had been openly taunted: "Well, General," a man calls out during inspection, "are you going to lead us to India next?"

Napoleon further alienates the men by turning on the rebel and answering disdainfully: "No, it is not with such men as you that I would conquer India . . ."

India is beside the point, except perhaps as a metaphor for the ends of the earth, the place where Alexander the Great's men finally mutinied and would go no further, an allusion that would not be lost on Napoleon. The real question is whether Napoleon can conquer and hold Egypt with "such men" who, for all their complaining, and despite their general's disdain, are truly heroic.

It is a question almost immediately answered, on that day in Rahmaniya when the French get their first sight of the Mamelukes. The entire army would have been annihilated when Murad bey suddenly appeared above the watermelon patches and the Nile were it not for the merest chance.

Looking up and seeing the huge, well-armed Mamelukes on their sleek horses, the Frenchmen despair. But lo and behold, Murad bey, after surveying the scene, retires. The Mameluke army the French imagine is behind him—just on the other side of the hills—is not there. Leaving his main force some miles away, Murad has come with only a scouting party, giving the Frenchmen time to scramble from the river, toss away their watermelons, and prepare to battle.

The next day, early in the morning, Napoleon leads his no-longer-naked men toward the encounter, switching from the defensive to the offensive. He seeks to engage the enemy in this isolated place as opposed to Cairo where, in case of a disaster, they would be able to fall back behind the walls of the great city.

Murad also undergoes a change, switching from the offensive to the defensive. Shortly after the French arrive, he sizes up the situation. After some preliminary fighting—little more than skirmishing—the wily Mameluke again retires, his warriors swiftly retreating on their Arabian mounts.

Made uneasy by unfamiliar French tactics, for the first time unsure of himself, Murad has no intention of fighting a decisive battle here. Let the French torturously make their way toward Cairo. There will be more heat, more unbearable thirst. The villages will be empty and the canals will be dry and surrounded by salt marshes. From tombs and ruins snipers will harass the foreigners . . . and they will arrive in Cairo ready for the slaughter.

⊓ ⊓ ⊓

Dawn, July 21, 1798. A plain before Cairo.

THROUGH THE HAZE of sand that grows thicker as the sun rises, the French soldiers can see the thousand mosques of Cairo in the far distance, their graceful minarets outlined against the brightening sky.

Closer to the battlefield, but still miles away, are those most ancient monuments, the pyramids, with their guardian: that colossus with its leonine torso and human face whom the Arabs call "Abu Hol," the Father of Terror; and whom the Greeks call Sphinx, or Strangler, for the death it exacts from those who can not guess the answer to its question; the riddle of our humanity.

Between its gigantic paws is the "plaque" of Thuthmosis IV (1400 BC). As a young prince hunting wild gazelle in the desert, he had fallen asleep here and dreamed that by clearing the creature of centuries of sand (it was more than a thousand years old even then) his reign would be blessed with a glory equal to his grandfather's, Thuthmosis III, the greatest warrior of Egypt.

Here war is a story as old as the pyramids of which the Arabs say: *All mortals are afraid of time, but Time is afraid of the pyramids.* When ancient Memphis, before Cairo, was the capital, then, too, great armies clashed on this plain.

Indeed, the scene Napoleon and his thirty-eight thousand Frenchmen have come to Egypt to enact has been played out here so often, that were it not for the modern guns and the European uniforms, the date might have been one, or two, or three, or four millennia before.

The very stars that have begun to fade overhead—the *Coma Berenike,* the tresses of Queen Berenice—take their name from just such a violent moment. War raged among the Ptolemies, and elephants brought from the heart of Africa trampled down men and clashed with one another. While these great beasts, maddened by the fumes of drugs and prodded on by their handlers (the "heavy artillery" of the day, each one equal to a thousand soldiers), a lovesick Queen, Berenike, cut off her beautiful hair and laid it on the altar of the gods, praying for victory for her husband.

She bequeaths to history a passionate story: how she killed her mother whom she found sleeping with her fiancé; and how she then came to Egypt and had fallen deeply in love with her new husband, Ptolemy III. "Brave girl, a splendid crime it was that won you your prince," the Alexandrian poet Callimachus sings.

More important than her story—for Champollion—she leaves behind her name: Berenike (or Berenice), one of the four royal Ptolemaic names, *Berenike, Arsinoe, Ptolemy, Cleopatra.* It will be repeated again and again, century after century, in various combinations and with sundry epithets, weaving a tapestry of sound that Champollion later unravels on obelisks and papyri and tombs and monuments.

What are the accidents by which our past is remembered! Berenike cuts off her beautiful hair to safeguard her husband's life and a priest at the temple steals it for his sensual pleasure! If the hair had not been stolen; if the queen had not found out about it (having taken her victorious husband to the temple to show him her sacrifice); if the royal couple, enraged, had not decreed death for all the priests (since which one was the fetishist-thief could not be determined); if the court astronomer Conan had not been so imaginative, if he had not saved the day by declaring that it was a god, none other, who had taken her flowing tresses and arranged them in the sky, would Champollion and his rival Thomas Young both have been so quick to guess that signified "Berenike"? Would her name—written not only on stone, but in the heavens as well—have so quickly come to mind?

The *Coma Berenike,* the hair of Berenice!

It is not only on the linguists, on Young and Champollion, that these ancient stars shed their light, but on the awed French soldiers as well. They feel the solemnity of the moment as they march across the vast, empty plain among the pyramids and tombs.

Call it awe, call it a dream or an illusion which takes hold of everyone here. Even in daylight, even when the sun comes out in all its strength and scorches both the victorious and the vanquished, even then the echoes of time can be heard and the weight of the past is palpable.

Marching quickstep—103 paces per minute and in close line formation—a unique feat achieved by Napoleon's severe discipline and drilling—the men prepare for battle.

"Soldiers!" Napoleon addresses them with a rhetoric as grand as the occasion requires: "From the height of these monuments, forty centuries of history look down upon you . . ."

There is the sound of trumpets and drums. The band begins to play the *Marseillaise,* but it is interrupted by the strange trilling of Oriental music, of tambourines and flutes, and savage battle cries.

Through the haze of sand and sunlight comes the sight of thousands upon thousands of men galloping across the plain on horseback. The Mamelukes have arrived.

ﾛ ﾛ ﾛ

"WHEN THEY FOUGHT an enemy, the Romans sought
to crush him with the weight of the world," Bonaparte had
told his generals beforehand. "We will do the same."

But as rank upon rank of splendid horsemen cross
the plain toward the waiting Frenchmen—Napoleon has
opted for a stationary line of defense in the face of Murad's
vastly superior cavalry—it seems suddenly that the "weight
of the world" is on the Mameluke's side.

Fall in! the cry goes up at the sight of Murad's troops, as
the moment for which Napoleon has been long preparing
arrives.

The men have already taken up their positions, the
infantry forming five large hedgehogs or squares six ranks
deep with heavy artillery (eighteen pounders) placed at
each of the corners.

Inside these squares are stationed the scanty and inade-
quate French cavalry, held in reserve. An order for them to
charge would be a futile last resort, they know, and would
only be given in the face of general disaster.

Napoleon has commanded that the men wait until the
galloping horsemen are mere paces away. They are to
remain immobile and unflinching in the face of the shock

THE LINGUIST AND THE EMPEROR

attack—the Mameluke specialty—and then they are to fire in unison, remaining in position for the next wave of riders.

The great question is whether the squares will hold in the face of the violent Mameluke charges.

"So furious was the Mameluke onslaught," the military historian, Harold, observes, "that the mortally wounded horses were carried by their sheer momentum inside the French ranks where they were finished off with bayonets and rifle butts . . . The least break in discipline [by the French] hundreds of miles south in this foreign country would have meant certain annihilation."

Again and again, the Mamelukes charge, daring and courageous in their desperation.

With the cries of the dying in their ears, with the booming of the guns and the exploding shells drowning out the commands of their officers and even the signals of the trumpets and drums, the Frenchmen stand fast.

If the strain on the French soldiers is terrible, the slaughter of the Mamelukes is equally merciless. Thousands fall in the first hour of the engagement alone, their bejeweled turbans and splendid swords glittering in the sun.

The French restraint is so complete that not even the rich booty tempts them from their squares.

Charge after charge fails until the Mameluke horsemen must leap over mounds of the dead. The "rabble" rounded up from Cairo and the hapless farmers, the *fellahin* with their clubs—also pressed into service—try to clear a path for the mounted warriors, but it is impossible.

As the day wears on, a mere remnant remains of the thirty thousand who at dawn had swaggered forth to war. It becomes obvious to the Mamelukes that the shabby-looking foreigners in their unglorious squares have cold-bloodedly won.

Dazed and broken, the survivors, Murad bey among them, begin to flee. They try to cross the Nile and return to Cairo from behind whose walls they hope to mount a defense.

Napoleon orders his men to pursue and the retreat becomes a massacre during which the death of the Mameluke leader Murad goes almost unnoticed. Desperate men crowd onto river boats that sink under their weight. Those who try to ford the river on horseback are easily picked off by the Frenchmen on shore.

One Frenchman holds back from the fray, sitting astride a camel and watching. He makes remarks to his young aide-de-campe, Josephine's son, speaking to him rapidly and harshly and with an Italian accent (for General Bonaparte is, after all is said and done, a Frenchman *by courtesy*).

Already, he is making plans for the occupation of Cairo, dictating notes about sanitary measures to prevent the plague; ways to light the dark city at night; and—almost as imperturbable as the Sphinx in whose presence the historic battle has been fought—he even has the sangfroid to consider, as the last of the Mamelukes either flee or drown, whether it will be feasible to build windmills along the banks of the Nile.

As an ironic postscript to the Battle of the Pyramids, it must be recorded that a solitary windmill *is* built. It will end up serving a far different purpose from the one Napoleon envisions. For in one of those strange genealogies of history, it will stand useless and futile at the outskirts of Cairo until the 1950s when the Coptic patriarch, forced out of his monastery by the socialist Nasser, takes up residence here.

From an upper chamber, the holy man blesses the faithful who flock to the windmill from all over Egypt. Beneath its unmoving arms, he chants prayers to the dog-headed saints who have replaced the dog-headed gods of Egypt. He takes in an army of beggars and lepers and tends to their needs, teaching, by example, a lesson Napoleon would have scorned: that the meek will inherit the earth. Or if not the earth, at least a ruin in a land that does not lack for ruins. For by the 1950s that is all that remains: the ruins of a windmill built by a general who is practical, ruthless, brilliant, and as mad as Don Quixote. A general who, for all his mistakes—and Egypt will be one of them—will be hailed as emperor.

But even as Napoleon proceeds toward Cairo, even as he

sketches plans for windmills and street lamps, Admiral Nelson is circling back to destroy the entire French fleet moored off Alexandria. Cutting off all means of supply to France's army, Nelson thus ensures that the French surrender in Egypt will only be a matter of time.

⌐ ⌐ ⌐

"ASK ME FOR an image of civilization," wrote the philosopher Seneca, "and I will give you the sack of a great city." This is what all Cairo fears as news of the disaster spreads: There is no one left to defend it.

Murad bey is dead and Ibrahim bey has headed south with his followers. Even the foreign soldiers of fortune—Greeks and Italians mostly—are gone, taking with them the sultan's emissary along with his pleasure boat. They disappear downriver where the foreign soldiers and the pasha and his troupe of singers and musicians and dancing girls are never heard from again.

Whoever is able to, flees. Many are cut down or enslaved by the Bedouins who await them in the desert. The rich and the poor, the young and the old, the healthy and the infirm all panic. Young boys lead blind Koran-reciters. Black eunuchs lead veiled harem-women along the way. Donkey carts filled with European treasures are dragged behind them: porcelain and mirrors and harps; and four-poster beds on which have been painted naked nymphs and obscene, lustful satyrs; and trompe-l'oeil cupids riding lions who roar with delight.

Whirling dervishes dance in the streets while store-houses are looted and prisons are emptied and mosques call the faithful to prayer.

⌐⌐ ⌐⌐ ⌐⌐

THE FALL OF Cairo makes the French masters of Egypt. Now Bonaparte's main conquest will be himself. He will try to forget Josephine and console himself with others, to recover from his loss and heal his wounded pride.

Of course he has responsibilities and decisions and duties. He is just as pressed as before. But though events continue to unfold with as much drama and intensity as before, the pattern remains the same.

A full-scale rebellion in Cairo, for example, is put down

with military severity: a cruelty surpassing even that of the Mamelukes which he had so deplored. There is a side campaign into Palestine, torturous and difficult from its beginning to its plague-ridden end.

But what does Napoleon think of as he enters the Tivoli: the theater and dance hall the French have created in Cairo for their pleasure?

Is it the demonically cunning Djezzar who had defeated him at Acre with the trick of a second wall? The first gave way and when the French poured through the breach, they were slaughtered in the enclosure.

Or does he recall the unaccountable rebellion of the Egyptians (whom he has treated so well, he exclaims)?

It is more likely that Napoleon muses over the woman at his side, the beautiful blond Pauline Fourès, the young wife of an artillery lieutenant. A stowaway who came to Egypt to be with her husband, she is nevertheless in her element with the general. He only turns to her after his disappointment in a series of dusky beauties, first local Egyptian girls (whose "imperfections" offend him); and then Abyssinian slaves with whom he tries to forget.

Still and all, women light or dark do not console him. He is bitter.

When General Bonaparte returns from Egypt, he locks himself in his room, giving strict instructions that Josephine not be allowed in the house.

Surprised by his sudden appearance in France, she is still on her way back to Paris. However, when she arrives, she brushes aside the servants, who are all on her side, and weeps all night before her husband's locked door. By morning, he has capitulated and forgiven her betrayal.

It is a well-known story. Josephine confides it to her close friends. Servants listen to everything behind their doors. Napoleon himself later recounts it to a courtier after everything is over—war and passion and glory—and he is living on the island of his exile. He adds with a rueful smile that he had inscribed *To Destiny* on the wedding brooch he gave her, not *To Love* . . .

For all his ruefulness, it is Josephine's name that is on his lips during his death agonies. It is "Josephine, divine Josephine" he calls for and not "the brood mare," as he refers to the Austrian archduchess he later marries, obsessed with founding a dynasty.

But to call for your beloved on a remote volcanic island during convulsions is one thing. To pay her bills when you are in a state of perfect health is another. For during her husband's absence in Egypt, the "divine" Josephine has been busy with more than romantic infidelities. She has spent some 1.5 million francs for dresses, jewels, and furnishings. She decides to keep this matter from Napoleon, having one of her friends in the government pay it with funds put aside for medical supplies for the army.

This comes to light, however—as financial subterfuges have a way of doing sooner or later (in this case, it is sooner)—during Bonaparte's second conquest of Italy. The "fools" at the Directory had lost Italy while he was away in Egypt, and now he must conquer it again. There are shortages of bandages and medicine and no hospital tents to ease the agonies of the dying. Napoleon is furious when he discovers why.

Denon, who continues to follow Napoleon after Egypt, helps calm him and shrug off the matter. The artist is grateful to Josephine, she has been a patroness of sorts, convincing the reluctant Napoleon to take Denon along on the Egyptian campaign and in general trying to help further the artist's career.

But it is not only a question of Denon's gratitude. His natural sympathy is in any case with Josephine, since his perspective is ancien régime. His milieu is the *bal des prostitués* where nobility mingle with the deliciously low, where all the whores of Paris, male and female, are guests of honor. What does a lover matter? What do two? And as for Josephine's extravagance, he argues, what could be more natural? Compared to that of others he has known, Madame Pompadour and Mme. du Barry and Marie Antoinette, it is nothing.

The artist proves a good advocate for her with the angry, wounded Napoleon, the older man relating a thousand and one tales of the courts where in his heyday he had been an intimate—those of Louis XV and Louis XVI, and of Catherine the Great and of Napoleon's fellow military genius and hero, Frederick the Great.

Denon holds up Frederick, completely indifferent to bourgeois morality, as a model. Told during a tour of inspection why a soldier was in chains—bestiality with a horse—Frederick's famous reply was: Fools! Put him in the cavalry! Denon also points to a Bourbon prince as an example of rational sangfroid. Finding his wife in bed with her lover, the royal merely turned away and murmured, *What, monsieur! Without being obliged?* Napoleon, however, is still too much the romantic—and the Italian—to take such matters lightly.

His ideal is a different sort completely. Earlier, when the aggressive, intellectual, and large-bosomed Madame de Staël had stalked him at one of Tallyrand's salons, gazing at him intently and asking: *Who do you consider the perfect woman, general?* Napoleon had replied without a pause: *My wife . . .*

The intellectual and politically astute de Staël does not attract him. He loves the faithless Josephine with a tempestuous, disappointed, angry love, though his ideal is something else again! It is the malleable and insipid Austrian archduchess he later marries, dutiful and docile and little more than a child. It is his innocent, wide-eyed Polish mistress, also little more than a girl.

It is an eternal "moment" he is smitten with: the moment when the frightened bride weeps in the (Aldobrandini) *Wedding:* an ancient fresco he becomes obsessed with bringing back to France, though Pius VII somehow manages to keep it in Rome.

In the painting, a curly-headed youth—the bridegroom's messenger?—leans against a wall, waiting as a sensual Venus, half-nude, sits next to the bride, comforting her, perhaps informing her of what is soon to be.

Josephine is not the bride of the ancient wedding. Still, she is able to hurt Napoleon as no one else can, to draw on deeply buried feelings in him.

After Egypt, he learns to love her again and to forgive her, reclaiming a part of himself which he, emperor and "Man of Destiny," is otherwise unable to acknowledge— his weakness, his humanity.

Chapter Twelve

The Divine
Crossword Puzzle

DURING THE REIGN of the "inglorious" Louis
XVIII, nothing is possible anymore, everything is over . . .
such is the feeling, the spiritual malaise, which settles over
France, over Europe.

While on a hot summer's afternoon in Egypt:

The French consul in Egypt, Bernadino Drovetti, an Italian by birth, sits in his wooden-frame house in Alexandria
conducting a hearing, a kind of preliminary investigation.
The surroundings are informal: the consul's small menagerie
runs wild in the garden—ostriches and baboons and a
giraffe (brought up from the Sudan by the naturalist St.
Hilaire and soon to become a celebrity in France as Europe's
first giraffe). Those who cannot crowd into the house listen
to the proceedings from the porch that surrounds the unim-
posing building, for this is a much-talked-about case.

The atmosphere is somber since, for all the informality of the surroundings, Drovetti's decision is binding and the case is one of life and death.

Strictly speaking, the consul is an unlikely man to serve as judge. Though he has studied law in his youth and therefore by default is better qualified to preside than the other foreign consuls, still he himself is, if rumors are to be believed, as criminal as the accused. This would be a certain Dr. Duzcap, an Italian who had run away from Istanbul with the wife of a wealthy Armenian banker and then possibly murdered her for her jewels.

While Drovetti, with his large mustache and terrible flashing eyes, judges Duzcap, trying to disentangle rumor from fact, the European community also judges the judge—in whispers, naturally, and with innuendos. Too powerful to confront openly, he is said to be involved in every kind of immoral scheme.

A dealer in antiquities, he is a man who manages to acquire great collections and then to sell them for a fortune—statues, papyri, jewelry. The collection in Turin which Champollion studies for months had been sold to the prince of Savoy by Drovetti, an immensely valuable collection like others the consul has offered for sale.

He will stop at nothing to get the pieces he wants, so it is said. His methods are deplorable. If twenty ancient alabaster vases are found in a tomb, he will see to it that half are smashed to bring up their price. If an obelisk catches his eye, he will have it hurled down and its pyramidion (top portion) broken off to make it easier to dispose of, etc.

Countless such stories circulate about him, along with rumors of his slave dealings: girls he brings from Ethiopia and eunuchs from the Sudan—young men captured from desert tribes and castrated by Coptic priests. More than half die while the survivors are sent to tend harems in Cairo.

But if Drovetti has many sins on his head, he remains a hero of sorts. Statues of him are raised in his native Italy, acknowledging the service he has performed in gathering together the magnificent works of Egyptian art and astonishingly beautiful papyri for Europe.

If he is despoiling Egypt, well, his admirers would say, consider the destruction visited on the antiquities by the Egyptians themselves. Indeed, Mohammed Ali, who rules Egypt after the French are forced out, desires to pull down the pyramids themselves in order to use their huge stones for the dams and canals he is building. He is only dissuaded by the difficulty he encounters in the attempt.

Drovetti has Mohammed Ali's ear: Will the statues and papyri bring a high price? Will they win the good will of European nations? The pasha is only too ready to dispose of them, just as a century earlier tons of pulverized mummies were shipped to Europe either as fertilizer or as a medicine for every ailment from gout to impotence.

From Turin, Champollion will write to Drovetti, asking about the provenance of various antiquities, not knowing that the place of origin has been purposely obscured to conceal the brigandage by which they were obtained.

While polite in his response to the awkward questions, Drovetti's civility masks a deep malice. Working behind the scenes, through a network of political friends, the consul will try to prevent Champollion's visit to Egypt.

When Champollion, circumventing him, finally does arrive in Egypt, Drovetti will try to prevent him from traveling down the Nile, creating all kinds of obstacles to keep him under his eye in Alexandria. Wherever Champollion goes, he is in the way. Champollion is forever stumbling into one or another of the "turfs" into which Egypt has been divided by the principal collectors: Drovetti; Henry Salt, the British consul; the German consul—harsh, greedy men and their Egyptian accomplices who conduct "business" with duplicity and violence.

". . . you will be pleased to hear of the discovery I made of a bilingual stone among Drovetti's things," Champollion's rival, Young, writes during a visit to Italy, "which promises to be invaluable."

Young engages an artist to copy the inscriptions on the object, but Drovetti denies him permission: "Drovetti's cupidity seems to have been roused . . . and he has given me to understand, that nothing should induce him to separate it from the remainder of his . . . collection, of which he thinks it so well calculated to enhance the price. He refuses to allow any kind of copy of it to be taken."

Thus the possibility of a great advance in the knowledge of the human past is turned into a familiar object of sordid barter: filthy lucre. As are moving and intimate images from the far distant past: a delicate carving of a queen playing on her game board with the god of Eternity . . . An inscription recalling an expedition to the eastern desert to quarry stone in which a gazelle giving birth is chanced upon and immediately sacrificed, together with her young, to the gods . . . The tale of Snefru, a pyramid-building pharaoh suffering from ennui five thousand years ago, asking his harem to become "sailors" and dressed in nothing but fish nets to row him about the sacred lake:

> . . . a pleasure though I found none. And Zazamonkh said: "If Your Majesty would take the beauties of the palace to the lake of the Great House . . . Then will the heart of your majesty be made joyous as they row to and fro . . . Then will happiness enter your heart . . ."

The rapacious foreign consuls—Drovetti foremost among them!—with their corrupt agents, feverish with greed, scavenge among the ruins—oblivious to death by plague or massacre in the lawless countryside, obsessed with gain as they gather their great collections: sphinxes and gods and demons, the sculptures which have lain under the sand for an eternity, the powerful, brooding faces of kings which the modern world will gaze upon with awe.

ꐒ ꐒ ꐒ

THE DECIPHERMENT BEGINS with a handful of "letters" thrown down on a page of Jean Francois' notebook—*Ptolemaios,* the Greek form of Ptolemy, next to the eight hieroglyphs encircled in the cartouche on the Rosetta stone: if the cartouche is encircling a foreign name, it stands to reason that these eight letters must spell Ptolemy:

P	■
T	◢
O	𝔰
L	⤛
M	=
AI	ᛁᛁ
S	ꓹ

Not only Champollion but Young had been working on the problem of the foreign names—or rather, the foreign "name" on the Rosetta stone, for there was only one of them, "Ptolemy."

Of the eight letters, Young got five of them right, but more important than conjecturing the value of a letter more or a letter less was Champollion's overall approach.

At this point, both men assume that only the names of foreign kings would have to be written with an alphabet in Egyptian. How else but phonetically could Ptolemy or Berenike or Xerxes or Darius, etc., be recorded?

The principle for indicating such sounds might be like that of a "rebus," Jean François conjectured. It would be as if when writing the English word "seer" one used a picture of the sea plus an "ear." Or as if "seersucker" was jotted down—as in a seersucker suit—by joining a bearded sage to a fool scratching his head—a sucker—and so on, using fertile, inventive combinations for every contingency.

Or, Champollion also opined, these special cases where phonetic writing was required might use the "acrophonic" principle—a "rabbit" for the letter "r," a door for the letter "d," etc.; the *initial* sounds of a word being indicated by its picture.

Apart from these foreign names, though, the pure hieroglyphs "depict the ideas and not the sounds of the language . . ." as Champollion puts it.

This far, there is general agreement. But Egyptian script is another matter. The script had been thought to be a different form of writing from the "pure" hieroglyphs, and what's more an alphabetic or phonetic one.

On the Rosetta stone, the Egyptian section made use of both hieroglyphs and "demotic" script, the latest and simplest form of cursive Egyptian. And there are also two other Egyptian scripts (not used on the Stone): the so-called "hieratic" or priestly script; and linear hieroglyphs, both simplifications of the detailed carvings and paintings on tombs and monuments. For example, *old man* in its four forms:

Now while Young never learned to distinguish between "demotic" and "hieratic" and probably never even realized that linear hieroglyphs existed, Champollion immersed himself in the scripts obsessively. Going back and forth between them, he finally came to realize that all four forms of writing operated on the same principle. Therefore, the scripts—like the pure hieroglyphs—could not be phonetic since the pure hieroglyphs were not. They were *not* an alphabet.

Champollion became so expert in recognizing the correspondences between the scripts, that he would transcribe words, whose meaning he still did not know, back and forth from cursive to hieroglyph and from hieroglyph to cursive, until, like Coptic, it became second nature to him.

This fluency in the scripts—along with his deep knowledge of Coptic—gets him over his next and perhaps most formidable hurdle. But before he can take that leap, first there is a vital piece of the puzzle which Fate or Chance must supply.

For up until this point, the eight letter/hieroglyphs which have been deciphered from the name of Ptolemy are only guesses or conjectures. In order to proceed according to sound linguistic principles, Champollion needs to cross-check them against a *second* ancient source. And like the Rosetta stone, this second source—whatever it might be—

must contain a known, foreign royal name other than Ptolemy—yet containing some of the same letters.

Even as Jean François wrestles with this problem, this second ancient source—a gift of the gods—has finally, after endless difficulties and delays lasting more than a decade, reached England.

ΓU ΓU ΓU

Granada, Spain. 1809.

WILLIAM BANKES was a member of parliament and lord of Kingston Lacy, one of the great landed estates in nineteenth-century England. A nobleman who usually took his place among statesmen and generals and royalty, on this hot July day in 1809, he could be seen lolling in the shady hills above Granada with a band of Gypsies.

He had not accompanied Wellington to fight the French in Portugal and Spain. Rather, he had come along to watch his countrymen fight the French, led by Napoleon's brother Joseph whom the Emperor has put in charge here.

As the campaign drags on, Bankes, aesthete and misfit, becomes bored and wanders off to consort with thieves and Gypsies in the south. For a while he gives himself up to all-night revelries and feasts of miscellaneous scraps including a "sublime ragout of cat," as he writes his friend, Lord Byron, "receipt [recipe] as follows . . ."

While thousands die in battle, in Spanish guerrilla actions and in brutal French reprisals, Bankes whiles away his time listening to love songs and having his fortune told by his new friends—none of whom will predict his actual fate: he will eventually be forced to flee England and live in exile to avoid imprisonment for "sexual depravity."

For the time being, his passions are not yet criminal (or not yet exposed as such). By the time Wellington has left Spain as a hero to pursue a woman who had rejected him years before, Bankes has also left Spain, and is also in pursuit of an ancient object of desire: a fallen obelisk on the island of Philae he has long dreamed of claiming for his own.

Bankes had begun to covet the massive monument from the moment he had first seen Denon's sketch of it in *The Description of Egypt* . . . as only a man of his means might covet a six-ton objet d'art—or as only the lord of Kingston Lacy might dream of transporting it from the remote island in the Nile where it had first been raised millennia before by that naturalist and bigamist Ptolemy VIII Physcon and his mother-daughter team of wives, Cleopatra II and Cleopatra III.

That there might be difficulties involved in bringing it to Kingston Lacy, even Bankes admits. But his determination only becomes stronger when, after making the long pilgrimage down the Nile, he finds the obelisk lying half covered with sand near a ruined temple.

In its original position, it would have soared skyward and shimmered with "electrum"—a gilding of white gold and silver long since stripped away by thieves. Even as it is— slender and graceful despite its weight; exquisitely carved and covered with hieroglyphs—it is more splendid and beautiful than he had imagined it.

Bankes stands before it lost in admiration, oblivious to the heat and the importunate beggars and clamorous guides surrounding him. What the monument once meant, what any of the obelisks could have meant for the Egyptians, he has no way of knowing. How could he—when even in antiquity the meaning of the obelisks had been forgotten? Even the ancient Romans brought the great monuments from Egypt in all ignorance. They had lashed the granite monoliths to three-tiered slave galleys, some of the obelisks two or even three times the size of the beauty which entranced Bankes. For the Romans, the obelisks are fitting symbols of the power, a world empire now passed to Rome.

Perhaps some old priest of Ra or Isis or Ptah, some living relic come to end his days in Rome, could explain the
Egyptian theology: how the god Ptah, in the beginning of
time, in darkness and solitude, had brought the world into
being by marrying his hand to his member . . . And thus in
the midst of the watery chaos called *nun,* a primeval mountain arose, formed of the god's semen. This divine act of
onanism is recorded by the obelisks which, recalling the
first mountain, soar and shimmer in the sun.

More likely, though, the priest himself would no longer
remember the ancient cosmogony. It is just one of many: a
hundred contradictory explanations of existence were proposed by the metaphysicians of Egypt, whose wisdom consisted of including them all.

But of what use would it be for the old priest—even
saying he remembered them—to try to explain the ancient
images and ideas? How much easier to make up a rigma-
role for any idle, rich Roman who cared to ask (and to pay
for the answer): a hodgepodge as meaningless as the fake
hieroglyphs sometimes found in Rome, copies of Egyptian
writing made by charlatans for curious Romans.

These copies—sometimes copies of copies—will be
unearthed long afterward, during the European Renaissance when the popes set chained criminals to digging in
the ruins of Rome. Thus, there will be spurious and corrupt specimens of the hieroglyphs for Renaissance scholars

to puzzle over . . . along with the authentic ones. The obelisks, hurled to the ground during barbarian invasions, have been raised once again by these same antiquity-hunting popes who now rule Rome in place of emperors. They crown them with crosses and sprinkle them with holy water and claim them in the name of Christ, though there is no mistaking the signs of the sun inscribed on them, or the profile of the jackal-headed Anubis, or the breasts of Hathor, goddess of pleasure and love.

⌐⌐ ⌐⌐ ⌐⌐

WHILE IN EGYPT, Bankes arranges a meeting with the Italian strongman Belzoni who has been scavenging among the ruins in the south. And for a price Belzoni promises to circumvent the two most dangerous of the foreign consuls in Egypt, Drovetti, acting for France, and Salt, acting for England.

Working in stealth and secrecy, Belzoni floats the massive obelisk hundreds of miles upriver to the coast and thence to England. He manages to accomplish this feat with a small army of Egyptian *fellahin* he recruits, despite the fact that boats sink and piers collapse under its weight and the precious object is almost lost in the Nile.

When it finally does arrive in England, no less a personage than Wellington will lay the foundation stone for its new base in Kingston Lacy. However, by the time the obelisk stands erect, pointing toward the sky, Bankes has fled England—one step ahead of the law.

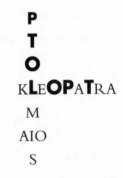

P
T
O
KLEOPATRA
M
AIO
S

The name *Kleopatra* is found inscribed in Greek on the broken-off pedestal of Bankes' obelisk; it is a name which provides the interlocking letters which should then appear in the hieroglyphs carved on the obelisk's side: the "L"; the "T"; the "O"; and the "E" = the "AI" or "Y" sounds

PTOLEMY, PTOLEMAIOS, PTOLMYS

KLEOPATRA

However, the , the "T" in Ptolemy is represented by a hand, , "T" in Cleopatra. It is not a major stumbling block, in any case, since more than one sign can represent the same sound, Champollion knows. He goes ahead and applies the twelve sounds he has now proven to other cartouches with interlocking letters.

For example, there are the letters he now knows from a cartouche reproduced in *The Description of Egypt*:

Al ____ SE ____ TRS

By simply adding a "K" and an "N" the cartouche would yield "Alksentros" or Alexander—for Alexander the Great (keeping in mind that in hieroglyphs the vowels would probably be irregularly indicated—sometimes present, sometimes left out, as in Hebrew or Arabic):

ALKSNDRS

Once again, however, there is a difficulty. There are two "S"s in Alexander's name. Sometimes they are both given by a double-bolt sign: . And sometime they are given as a folded cloth or bent scepter, the way the "S" is

indicated in the Ptolemy cartouche: .

Champollion allows for the possibility of homophones, or two different signs expressing the same sound, in this case "S."

He leaves the realm of speculation, though, when he comes to the interlocking "K" of Kleopatra, a semicircle

or loaf of bread: ; and the "K" of Alexander, a basket

with a handle:  .

For here his knowledge of the scripts comes into play and he realizes that the demotic script form of the bread-loaf "K" in Cleopatra's name equaled a hieratic script sign which in turn equaled the "K"-basket-with-handle sign in Alexander's name.

In this way Champollion, unlike Young, proves, and does not merely guess, the existence of homophones—a fact that will eventually account for the huge numbers of letters found in the hieroglyphic alphabet.

Furthermore, he can be reasonably sure that the bread-loaf sign always seen in feminine names would = TE in Coptic, "the" (the feminine form of the article). Again drawing on his wide knowledge of Coptic, he makes the claim that the hand-sign which equals "T" is related to the Coptic word for hand, *TOT*—another example of the way in which initial sounds of words are used as letters (the "acrophonic" principle).

With this established, Champollion goes on to decipher a long list of Greek and Roman cartouches, increasing the letters of his Egyptian alphabet to over forty hieroglyphs which—he still believes—are used only for the writing of foreign names.

But Champollion begins to reconsider: there are five hundred words in the Greek section of the Rosetta stone corresponding to 1,419 hieroglyphic signs in the Egyptian section. If the hieroglyphs each stood for a single word, it would make for a great disproportion.

More important, using his alphabet of hieroglyphs to

sound out groups of hieroglyphs, he begins to notice grammatical constructions as he pores over copies of the cartouches inscribed on the obelisks of Rome.

Domition his father Vespasian is written on the obelisk in the Piazza Navona—the hieroglyphic possessive form the same as the Coptic. Champollion considers the horned viper, the letter "F" in hieroglyphics— .

In linear hieroglyphics:

In hieratic:

In demotic:

In Coptic:

It is a letter whose shape and sound not only has remained constant for more than three thousand years but whose function—it is the third person pronoun in both Coptic and ancient Egyptian—remains the same.

In hieroglyphic texts even outside of the cartouches, in texts which could not be foreign names, certain signs—like the horned viper—are encountered again and again, with surprising frequency. If these hieroglyphs are sounds, letters expressing grammatical principles, if they are alphabetical, wouldn't it mean—couldn't it be—that the hieroglyphs constitute an alphabet after all, at least in part?

That would account for the frequent repetition of a limited number of signs, a core, scattered among the many hieroglyphic symbols—they would be words like "his" or pronouns, or negations.

Thus, letter by letter, the puzzle of the hieroglyphs is solved. Writing, fragile as a spider's web and strong as an iron chain, links centuries and millennia of existence. *Domitian* his *father Vespasian. Domitian* his *brother Titus*—the cruel, vain Roman emperor (obsessed with his thinning hair!) chooses to preserve his Roman name in Egyptian symbols on an obelisk. More than a thousand years later, Innocent X will raise the fallen monument and call it by his family name: the Pamphili obelisk. A famed Jesuit scholar, Athanasius Kircher, will misinterpret the writing on it, leaving behind many "learned" volumes of absurdities. And two hundred years later, Jean François will come to study in Rome and he will stand in Piazza Navonna, the square where gladiators once fought and Christian saints died. Champollion will gaze at the obelisk as they had. He will contemplate it by day and by night. And he will struggle with the hieroglyphs covering its sides, writing which gives form to the chaos of existence and expression to the terror of time.

口 口 口

EIGHT HUNDRED MILES to the south of Cairo—on the
border of the Sudan—the strongman Belzoni spends week
after week, month after month, supervising his *fellahin* as they
clear Ramesses' great temple at Abu Simbel, together with
the pyramids the most colossal monument in all Egypt. And
as the peasants cart away the desert sand, Belzoni sketches
whatever images and inscriptions come to light. One of his
sketches finds its way back to Europe in a letter; and a copy
of this copy finds its way to Jean François' attic room in Paris.

It contains a cartouche that Champollion has never seen
before:

The first symbol was the sun, that was clear; and in Coptic
the word for sun was Ra. That would give him, Ra___SS,
using the alphabet he had developed from the Ptolemaic
and Roman cartouches. And of course, by reading

as "M" or "Mes" that would be the famed pharaoh

Ramesses, he realizes, whose name had been recorded by the Greeks and Romans.

He begins to tremble with excitement. Here was an *ancient* pharaoh, an *Egyptian* pharaoh whose name was written in phonetic symbols, in letters, in the same way that the names of foreign kings were written. Champollion searches frantically through the rest of the Abu Simbel papers, looking for another cartouche to confirm what he already knows is true. There, among the sketches of the toiling *fellahin* and gigantic temple pillars, is another unfamiliar cartouche:

Leaving out the first symbol, it would be read ____MeSS. But the Ibis he already knew. A god, Thoth, this was another name the Greeks and the Romans had kept alive. The god of writing. And the cartouche therefore read "Thuthmosis." This was the most famous warrior in ancient Egypt, Ramesses' hero, the Napoleon of ancient Egypt, whose empire stretched from Megiddo to Cush.

◻ ◻ ◻

LATER, CHAMPOLLION WILL write of the hieroglyphs: "It is a complex system, a writing that is pictorial, symbolic and phonetic at one and the same time, in a single text, a single phrase and even in a single word. Each of these types of character aids in the notation of ideas by different means: It is a code."

As he refines his understanding, he identifies many different aspects of the writing. "Determinatives"—for example, non-phonetic indicators as to what order of being a word belonged. So that a hieroglyph to which a small bird was added (a determinative) took on a negative or evil or sickly connation; whereas that same hieroglyph with a small flag would indicate divinity. A wavy line was the determinative for liquid; a phallus emitting liquid, procreation; a forearm with a stick, force—and so on.

Champollion will work with *hapax legomena* (words connected to a specific time or subject, such as our "Watergate"). He toils over foreign words, Aramaic or Hebrew, embedded in Egyptian. He suffers the agonies of the damned deciphering ancient classics which only existed in the careless practice copies of schoolboys.

In defense of his decipherment, he will travel to Egypt and find hundreds upon hundreds of examples of writing to prove his discovery—which, like every great discovery, must go against tenaciously held ideas. Like Columbus, who was forced to controvert known fact, Champollion rejects the givens of the linguistic world, and presents a far-fetched theory of an ancient language endlessly complicated and rich and subtle: "visual poetry," he will call it, an interweaving of thought and image, of writing *and* sound.

But first—before he does any of this—he must run through the streets of Paris to tell his brother. And then he lies in a faint, in a coma. For eight days, he remains in a drugged dream.

After all, how can he bear it? It's a wonder it doesn't kill him! How can anyone bear such joy?

Epilogue

HONORS ARE BESTOWED upon Champollion from all sides. The pope, the French king, learned societies, universities, all extol his achievement. But Champollion views such praise only as a means to an end. Having the ear of the world, he can plead for more care in the excavation of the ancient sites of Egypt. Funds are made available for an Egyptian wing in the Louvre. A chair of Egyptology is established in the University of Paris.

There is still much work to be done, many mysteries of the ancient language to be unraveled. Yet with Champollion's decipherment, knowledge of our shared past is extended to include the long-silent millennia before Christ.

CHAMPOLLION RETURNS TO France from his researches in Egypt in the dead of winter. Perhaps with Drovetti's connivance, his boat is made to remain in quarantine outside of Marseille an extraordinary forty-two days. Not longer after, Champollion, at the height of his powers, dies at forty years of age.

His brother spends the next three decades editing and posthumously publishing his work.

Napoleon dies at fifty-two on St. Helena of arsenic poisoning. He will lie under a blank tombstone until 1840 when political circumstances permit the French, who will never forget him, to bring his body back.

And who are they, this improbable pair?

They are eternal types who have always existed and who always will.

Author's Note

TERENCE DUQUESNE'S essays are not only learned but filled with remarkable insights. I was particularly inspired by his "A Coptic Initiatory Invocation; An Essay in Interpretation with Critical Text" (PGM IV 1–25). Translation and commentary by Terence DuQuesne. Darengo, ThameOxon, 1991.

For those readers interested in further Coptic readings, I refer them to the superb collection, *Coptic Texts of Ritual Power,* edited by Marvin Meyer and Richard Smith.

For the often debated issue of early Egyptian cannibalism, I refer the reader to E. A. Wallis Budge's *Osiris and the Egyptian Resurrection,* to Sir William Flinders Petrie, and to the ancient writer Plutarch.

The ancient soldier's lament given in chapter 9 exists in

several versions. I refer the reader to Sir Alan H. Gardiner's excellent *Late Egyptian Miscellanies.* Brussels, 1937.

Although the poem by Archilochus (now among the Cologne Museum's collection of papyri) was discovered as a complete text only in 1916, bits and pieces surfaced earlier during various excavations.

Al Jabarti's *Chronicle of the French Occupation in Egypt* can be found in toto in a very readable edition brought out by Markus Wiener Publishers.

A reader interested in pursuing ancient Egyptian customs and habits can have no better guide than *The Mummy: A Handbook of Egyptian Funerary Archaeology* by E. A. Wallis Budge and *Ancient Lives* by John Romer.

Among the many texts consulted, I would particularly like to acknowledge my debt to Kenneth Burke, whose excellent introduction to *The Oresteia* is the source for my remarks about Aeschylus' trilogy.

For a comprehensive selection of early, middle, and late Egyptian texts, the reader is referred to *Ancient Egyptian Literature.* Vols. 1, 2, 3. University of California Press.

Those who would like to see events through the artist Denon's eyes will find his memoirs interesting reading: *Voyages dans la Basse et la Haute Egypte pendant les campagnes de Bonaparte en 1798 et 1799.* 2 vols. London, 1807.

For those who enjoy reading primary texts, it is possible to enjoy the newspaper which the French published in

Egypt, *Le Courrier de l'Egypte*. They will also be interested in such works as: *Copies of Original Letters from the Army of General Bonaparte in Egypt, Intercepted by the Fleet Under the Command of Admiral Lord Nelson*. London, 1798. *Correspondance de Napoleon I publiee par ordre de l'Empereur Napoleon III*. 32 vols. Paris, 1858–70. *Correspondance inedite, officielle et confidentielle de Napoleon Bonaparte*. Vols. V–VII. Egypte. 3 vols. Paris, 1819–20. And *Lettres de Napoleon à Josephine*. Edited by Leon Cerf. Paris, 1929.

And of course, there is the famous *Description de l'Egypte*, which can be found in many versions from the twenty-four-volume edition published in Paris, 1809–1828, to modern selections such as a recent one-volume paperback published by Taschen Books with very good illustrations.